EDWARD A. BUNYARD

THE ANATOMY
OF DESSERT

WITH A FEW NOTES ON WINE

RUTH REICHL
SERIES EDITOR

Introduction by Michael Pollan

Preface by David Karp

THE MODERN LIBRARY

NEW YORK

2006 Modern Library Paperback Edition

Introduction copyright © 2006 Michael Pollan
Preface copyright © 2006 David Karp
Series Introduction copyright © 2005 Ruth Reichl
All rights reserved.

Published in the United States by Modern Library, an imprint of The Random House
Publishing Group, a division of Random House, Inc., New York.

MODERN LIBRARY and the TORCHBEARER Design are registered trademarks of
Random House, Inc.

This edition is published by arrangement with E. P. Dutton & Co., Inc.,
a member of Penguin Group (USA), Inc.

LIBRARY OF CONGRESS CATALOGING-IN-PUBLICATION DATA
Bunyard, Edward A. (Edward Ashdown)
The anatomy of dessert : with a few notes on wine / Edward A. Bunyard.
p. cm.—(Modern Library food series)
Originally published: London : Dulau, 1929.
Includes index.

ISBN 0-8129-7157-4
1. Fruit.   2. Wine and wine making.   I. Title.   II. Modern Library food.
TX397.B8 2006
641.3′4—dc22   2006041882

www.modernlibrary.com

THE ANATOMY
OF DESSERT

INTRODUCTION TO THE MODERN LIBRARY FOOD SERIES

Ruth Reichl

My parents thought food was boring. This may explain why I began collecting cookbooks when I was very young. But although rebellion initially inspired my collection, economics and my mother's passion fueled it.

My mother was one of those people who found bargains irresistible. This meant she came screeching to a halt whenever she saw a tag sale, flea market, or secondhand store. While she scoured the tables, ever optimistic about finding a Steuben vase with only a small scratch, an overlooked piece of sterling, or even a lost Vermeer, I went off to inspect the cookbooks. In those days nobody was much interested in old cookbooks and you could get just about anything for a dime.

I bought piles of them and brought them home to pore over wonderful old pictures and read elaborate descriptions of dishes I could only imagine. I spent hours with my cookbooks, liking the taste of the words in my mouth as I lovingly repeated the names of exotic sauces: soubise, Mornay, dugléré. These things were never seen around our house.

As my collection grew, my parents became increasingly baffled. "Half of those cookbooks you find so compelling," my mother complained, "are absolutely useless. The recipes are so old you couldn't possibly use them."

How could I make her understand? I was not just reading recipes. To me, the books were filled with ghosts. History books left me cold, but I had only to open an old cookbook to find myself standing in some other place or time. "Listen to this," I said, opening an old tome with suggestions for dinner on a hot summer evening. I read the first recipe, an appetizer made of lemon gelatin poured into a banana skin filled with little banana balls. "When opened, the banana looks like a mammoth yellow pea pod," I concluded triumphantly. "Can you imagine a world in which that sounds like a good idea?" I could. I could put myself in the dining room with its fussy papered walls and hot air. I could see the maid carrying in this masterpiece, hear the exclamations of pleasure from the tightly corseted woman of the house.

But the magic didn't work for Mom; to her this particular doorway to history was closed. So I tried again, choosing something more exotic. "Listen to this," I said, and began reading. " 'Wild strawberries were at their peak in the adjacent forests at this particular moment, and we bought baskets of them promiscuously from the picturesque old denizens of the woods who picked them in the early dawn and hawked them from door to door.... The pastry was hot and crisp and the whole thing was permeated with a mysterious perfume.... Accompanied by a cool Vouvray...these wild strawberry tarts brought an indescribable sense of well-being....'

"Anything?" I asked. She shook her head.

Once I tried reading a passage from my very favorite old cookbook, a memoir by a famous chef who was raised in a small village in the south of France. In this story he recalls being sent to the butcher when he was a small boy. As I read I was transported to Provence at the end of the nineteenth century. I could see the village with its small stone houses and muddy streets. I could count the loaves of bread lined up at the *boulangerie* and watch the old men hunched over glasses of red wine at the café. I was right there in the kitchen as the boy handed the carefully wrapped morsel of meat to his mother, and I watched her put it into the pot hanging in the big fireplace. It sizzled; it was so real to me that I could actually smell the daube. My mother could not.

But then she was equally baffled by my passion for markets. I could stand for hours in the grocery store watching what people piled into their carts. "I can look through the food," I'd try to explain. "Just by paying attention to what people buy you can tell an awful lot about them." I would stand there, pointing out who was having hard times, who was religious, who lived alone. None of this interested my mother very much, but I found it fascinating.

In time, I came to understand that for people who really love it, food is a lens through which to view the world. For us, the way that people cook and eat, how they set their tables, and the utensils that they use all tell a story. If you choose to pay attention, cooking is an important cultural artifact, an expression of time, place, and personality.

I know hundreds of great cookbooks that deserve to be rescued from oblivion, but the ones I have chosen for the Modern Library Food Series are all very special, for they each offer more than recipes. You can certainly cook from these books, but you can also read through the recipes to the lives behind them. These are books for cooks and armchair cooks, for historians, for people who believe that what people eat—and why—is important.

Two are books I once read to my mother. *Clémentine in the Kitchen* introduces one of the most lovable and entertaining characters who ever picked up a whisk. She is the ultimate *bonne femme* and a nostalgic reminder of a long-gone life when people were truly connected to the land.

Life à la Henri, the memoir of the man who invented crêpes suzette, is more than a memoir and more than a cookbook; in the nearly one hundred years that he was alive, Henri Charpentier watched the world and its food change on two continents. He fed both Queen Victoria and Marilyn Monroe, he made and lost fortunes, and he never lost his sense of humor. I have been in love with Henri for most of my life, and I think it is time the rest of the world got to meet him.

Although Edouard de Pomiane must have breathed the same air as Henri Charpentier, they seem to belong to different ages. Henri's world is long gone, but Edouard de Pomiane seems thoroughly modern. If he turned up tomorrow in a time machine, he would be right at home. His first book, *Cooking with Pomiane,* was published in Paris in the thirties. It became Elizabeth David's favorite cookbook, and I find it hard to understand why it is not on every cook's shelf. If you forced me to depend on a single cookbook for the rest of my life, it would probably be this one, if only because having made the acquaintance of M. de Pomiane I am reluctant to lose his companionship. His book is filled with common sense, good humor, great writing, and wonderful recipes. It says a great deal, I think, that another book by this forgotten writer, *Cooking in Ten Minutes* (published in 1930), is probably the most widely imitated cookbook of our time.

The other astonishingly modern book in this series is *The Unprejudiced Palate,* which was written in 1948 but reads as if it just rolled off the presses. Angelo Pellegrini, cook, gardener, professor of English literature, and one of the most opinionated people who ever lived, must have been an amazement to his Seattle neighbors. He turned his lawn into a garden, grew much of his own food, advocated eating locally and seasonally, and generally invented what we have come to think of as the American food revolution fifty years before it ever happened.

The recipes in his book are so up-to-date that they make you reconsider everything you thought you knew about postwar America.

He gives recipes for pasta al pesto, for homemade sausage, for grilled steak. And just listen to what Pellegrini considered a suitable salad: "With the first spring crop fill your bowl with leaf lettuce and romaine or the first tender leaves of chicory. In the fall, fill the bowl with endive or escarole. Add to all of them a bit of minced parsley and watercress." Dressing? He suggested good olive oil, salt, pepper, and wine vinegar, along with garlic croutons.

Remember that this was at a time when most Americans bought olive oil, if they bought it at all, at the drugstore, and many were content to think of salad as half a canned peach filled with cottage cheese—or, as we learn from *Perfection Salad*, a few toasted marshmallows stuffed with raisins.

Did we ever live in a world in which women spent their time stuffing marshmallows with raisins? Apparently. One hundred years ago, in a frantic effort to control food and keep it in its place, American women were busily transforming the act of cooking into "domestic science." Laura Shapiro went back to recipes in old magazines and cookbooks to find out what those women were up to. It is a tragic tale that has had enormous repercussions for all of us. Still, the first time I read *Perfection Salad* I had only one thought: I wish my mom could read this.

I imagine myself handing this book over to my mother. "Okay," I would say, "I'll admit it. Food is sometimes boring." But then I'd tell her about those raisin-stuffed marshmallows and add, "But cookbooks never are."

CONTENTS

Introduction

Michael Pollan

"There are only ten minutes in the life of a pear when it is perfect to eat," Ralph Waldo Emerson observed. *The Anatomy of Dessert* concerns itself, to the point of obsession, with those ten minutes of fleeting deliciousness. Which, when you think about it, is no small thing in life—in fact is one of the secrets thereof, as Emerson understood. Actually Edward Bunyard, *The Anatomy*'s author, would probably regard a ten-minute window of perfection as a tad too generous. Attempting to pinpoint the optimal moment to eat gooseberries, he narrowed it down even further: "The moment of moments and day of days is on the return from church at 12:30 on a warm July day when the fruit is distinctly warm."

Though Bunyard's impassioned A-to-Z of fruits did not appear until 1929, several decades too late for Emerson to have savored it, the sage of Concord would surely have approved of its author's devotion to the nick of time, and also of his conviction that the fruits which nature gives us, no culture or cookery can improve. Indeed, you finish this book convinced that introducing a piece of well-grown ripe fruit to something as crass as flour or butter or—perish the thought!—*heat* is decadent at best and possibly sacrilegious.

When I first picked up Bunyard's book and realized its subject was not cakes and tarts and sorbets and such, but fruit plain and simple, I interpreted his title as a slap to the pastry chefs of the world, to their hubris in assuming that culinary artifice could hope to enhance what nature had already perfected. I decided Bunyard's *Anatomy* supplied the philosophical rationale for the stark copper bowl of unembellished ripe fruit that is always on the menu at Chez Panisse, an audacity that immediately endeared that restaurant to me. This presentation of the perfect Warren pear or Kishu tangerine or Bahri date has long been Alice Waters's way of saying that the true genius resides in the farmer who grew the thing; the chef merely celebrates that genius by seizing on the moment of moments and setting it off between the quotation marks of a menu. Ripeness is all.

A pretty conceit, but almost certainly not what Mr. Bunyard had in mind. You see, Bunyard was an Englishman, a nurseryman and connoisseur (of wine as well as fruit), and in the often eccentric dialect of English that is spoken in Great Britain, "dessert" is the word for "a serving of fresh fruit after the main course of a meal"; all that other pastry-chef stuff goes under the rubric of puddings or sweets. Oh well. But I still think Edward Bunyard would heartily approve of the copper fruit bowl at Chez Panisse, would second its eloquent statement on the relative merits of nature and art.

Bunyard would endorse, too, the contemporary cults of seasonality and the heirloom species, cults for which *The Anatomy of Dessert* could ably serve as Torah. Each of the book's chapters is consecrated to a single fruit, and after laying down a few vivid strokes of characterization ("The nectarine is a smooth peach, a peach which has lost its *duvet*"), Bunyard proceeds to unfurl the calendar of that fruit's important cultivars as they ripen week by week through the season, from July's scarlet Cardinal and Early Rivers to

August's Lord Napier and Humboldt ("just touched red at the stone") to the honeyed yellowy nectarines of September: Darwin, Pitmaston Orange, Spenser, and Victoria. Sad to say, a great many of the cultivars Bunyard so lovingly catalogs are long gone from commerce, if not extinct from nature (though happily, a handful are once again available as heirlooms in specialty nurseries). To read the book today is to realize how sadly diminished our world of fruit has grown, its spectacular biodiversity having been sacrificed on the altars of standardization, marketing, and long-distance freight.

Even in 1929, Bunyard recognized that the full banquet of fruity delights is available only to the gardener, who alone is in a position to give his pears, plums, and apricots the scrupulous attentions they require to achieve perfection. (He offers his condolences to "our town dwellers, who know so little of fruit at its best.") Here is his advice for the storing and treatment of Comice pears "in the fruit-room":*

The fruits should not even touch, much less should they be piled. The temperature of a cellar is about right for them. When the green colour begins to change to yellow the moment of watchfulness arises, and when the whole fruit is an even yellow the moment has arrived. As not all the fruits will arrive at this point simultaneously, great care is necessary, and no day should pass without inspection, but not handling.

This waiting game, the drawn-out foreplay of cultivation and inspection building up to the climactic first bite, is what really engages Bunyard about fruit, the erotics of which are never far beneath the surface of his occasionally extravagant Edwardian prose: "It is in this quiet carnal anticipating that much of the charm of fruit growing rests—as we watch the slow processes of development, the fugitive flower, its hope and fear, the slow swelling of the

*What? You have no fruit-room?!

fruit and the danger it runs, until we have for the survivors an almost maternal love...." *Maternal*, eh? This is not the only instance of barely sublimated fruit lust you will encounter in Bunyard's treatise.

But though Bunyard can certainly wax purple, he deplores the merely sweet, insisting on a measure of acid in both his fruit and his prose. The charm of pears "lies in a due proportion of acidity, and mere musk alone is to most palates an abomination." The man is nothing if not opinionated, and his raptures of ripeness never blind him to the inevitable disappointments of fruit, also, alas, a fact of life. Melons especially are apt to disillusion: "Of all the ideals which our poor humanity cherishes, the concept of the ideal Melon stands alone, for we know in our inmost souls that it will never be realised." You get the feeling Bunyard has been let down by a melon more times in his life than he'd care to admit, and he's loath to invest much more in that particular relationship; the melon chapter is comparatively brief and emotionally guarded.

Bunyard's passionate engagement with his subject is catching; you finish this book hungry for fresh fruit, though perhaps dubious that Bunyardian transports of delight await you in your supermarket's produce section. (They don't. You're much better off looking in the farmer's market, where you stand a better chance of catching the moment of moments and day of days.) His ardor reminds me of the steam that often rises from the prose of the rosarian or peony lover, men (they're usually men) in the grip of a similar botanical love affair. You certainly do not find this sort of prose expended upon the vegetable kingdom—who will ever extol "the tender femininities" of broccoli or "the Hanoverian lustiness" of the turnip?

That such passion is reserved for fruit and flowers makes perfect evolutionary sense. Fruit and flowers have both evolved with precisely this aim in view: to seduce animals so that we credulous humans might spread their genes, help them be fruitful and multiply. So the lusciousness of the plum and the voluptuousness of the apricot are no accidents or mere conceits; written down in DNA, these charms exist expressly to excite mammalian senses—to sweep us off our feet. All of us fall for fruit to one degree or another, but seldom has a human fallen quite as hard as Edward Bunyard did. In him fruit found its greatest lover.

PREFACE

David Karp

It is astonishing that the greatest book in English on fruit, revered by fruit connoisseurs as their bible, has been out of print for seventy years. Publishers doubtless presumed that few readers would buy a work chiefly describing obsolete fruit varieties, but while horticultural treatises are usually dry and narrowly focused, *The Anatomy of Dessert* represents a unique blend of pomology and belles lettres.

Its multifaceted appeal was enriched by the distinguished career and diverse interests of the author, Edward Ashdown Bunyard. Born in 1878 at Maidstone, in Kent, he was privately educated for reasons of health. In 1896 he started working for his family's renowned century-old nursery, which grew eight hundred varieties of fruit trees and had royal warrants to supply the court. On the death of his father, George (also a noted horticultural author), in 1919, he took over as principal of the firm, and was soon celebrated not only as Britain's leading pomologist but also as a rosarian, historian, bibliophile, and passionate epicure.

The author of hundreds of articles both scholarly and popular,

Bunyard founded and for several years edited the *Journal of Pomology*. He was a leading member of the Royal Horticultural Society, and helped set up the commercial fruit trials at the society's garden at Wisley. He was more interested in history and aesthetics than commerce, however. In financial straits, and despondent at the outbreak of war, he shot himself in his room at the Royal Societies Club on October 19, 1939. The stigma of suicide, alas, depressed interest in his life and work.

Bunyard wrote three other books: *A Handbook of Hardy Fruits* (in two volumes, 1920 and 1925); *Old Garden Roses* (1936); and, with the collaboration of his sister Lorna, *The Epicure's Companion* (1937). By far his best-known work, however, is *The Anatomy of Dessert,* written by 1924 and first published in 1929 in a signed, limited edition by Dulau & Company, horticultural booksellers in Old Bond Street. The second edition (1933) added "A Few Notes on Wine," and an American impression appeared the next year. Last reprinted in 1936, the book has long been prized by collectors.

Curiously for the American reader, the "Dessert" of the title, according to British use, specifically denotes fruit. "Anatomy" here connotes analysis and appreciation, founded on Bunyard's prodigious knowledge, interpreted by stringent critical standards. As the American preface declares, his "object is to show the range and variety of our resources and to emphasise very firmly that to have the best fruit you must grow it yourself."

The book depicts the passing of an era when gardeners for the wealthy grew fine fruit on great estates, often in greenhouses, and when gentlemen might bond over rare pears, as they would today over golf. Bunyard lamented that "these glories are fading in these unromantic days, when it is found 'cheaper to buy a bunch now and then from the stores.' " He delights in trenchant, provocative opinions, which sometimes, as in his snarky comments on America and his contempt for watermelon eaters, betray the prejudices of his class.

In each chapter Bunyard evokes the essence of a fruit, and describes, in seasonal order, its notable varieties, imparting to each a distinctive personality. He particularly esteems "high flavor," the intensity beloved by Victorian connoisseurs, but now a quaint notion in our age of fast fruit. Many of Bunyard's favorites are no longer grown even in England, but others such as Gravenstein apple and Comice pear are still widely available. In either case, readers may apprehend through Bunyard's judgments the qualities of fruit at its best.

The book's status as a classic transcends fruit, however, resting on its sensuous, lyrical style, imbued with peculiarly dry British wit, and graced by learned allusions, sometimes obscure but always delightful. Savor, for example, his rhapsodic portrait of the Transparent Gage: "a slight flush of red and then one looks into the depths of transparent amber as one looks into an opal, uncertain how far the eye can penetrate." Above all, Bunyard expresses an eminently civilized philosophy, epicurean in the classic sense, inquisitive and individualist, shunning the garish, and favoring temperate enjoyment of life's pleasures.

In the last decade, in reaction to the blandness of modern commercial fruit, interest in older and fuller-flavored varieties has burgeoned, inspiring enthusiasm for Bunyard's work. Two English scholars, Edward Wilson and Joan Morgan (to whom I am grateful for their generous help), have written articles illuminating the hitherto obscure details of Bunyard's life, and Mr. Wilson is editing a commemorative collection of essays, entitled *The Downright Epicure*, for Prospect Books. I hope that this reissue of Bunyard's masterpiece helps broaden the cult of his admirers.

PREFACE TO
THE AMERICAN EDITION

Edward A. Bunyard

It is a great moment for any author, especially to one of more than average modesty, when, with clear sheet of paper before him and poised pen, he writes the first words of a preface to an American Edition.

Shall I adopt those ringing accents, those majestic periods with which the chosen representatives of one race are wont to use in addressing another?

Happily it soon occurs to me that it is not the nation that I am approaching, but our very old friend, the gentle reader. Let us dine together; and with the dessert discuss our preface.

"Wine? Thank you, I will."

Now for this little book of mine. You will see it is mainly about fruit and its object is to show the range and variety of our resources and to emphasise very firmly that to have the best fruit you must grow it yourself.

The varieties which are grown in large quantities must first of all travel well to the markets and secondly crop well enough to pay someone to grow them. Now in England, as I imagine with you, it does not always happen that the best flavour is combined with such qualities. We therefore must rely on the home garden for the best and it is only here that we can gather them at the moment of perfection.

Nearly all the Plums, Cherries and Pears described here have been successfully grown in New York State. For the Gooseberries I fear you must come to England, hot sun and dry summers are its enemies. Our Strawberries, as you will find hereafter, are of American descent.

One of the first things that Capt. John Smith noted on landing in Virginia were "fine and beautiful Strawberries, foure times bigger and better than ones in England." Whether the same can be said today I cannot decide, preferring quality to size I choose the descendants of the smaller Virginian Strawberry, such as Black Prince.

Grapes ("Thank you, I will") we grow in England in glass houses, and lavish on them no less care than our orchids. The quality of the American Grape I must take on trust, but I have the trustworthy evidence of their excellence.

As for wine, for long California sent its surplus to England and may perhaps do so again though the quite legitimate leeway of home consumption has been taken up.

I am glad to know that the great wines of France and Germany are not strangers to your shores, they speak a common language to us all and civilisation has found no firmer bond than that of mutual tastes.

"Port?"

"Thank you, I will."

Fruit, like man, is a creature of environment and to each country is given certain advantages. America I have never visited but, thanks to an unceasing flow of Bulletins from agricultural colleges, I know probably as much of the mean rainfall of Wisconsin as you do.

From Miami to Cape Flattery I have journeyed with your authors, with Thoreau (rather dry), with Jack London (somewhat wet). Walt Whitman introduced me to the Seckle Pear and, making a leap, Gertrude Atherton to Boston. Have I done wrong in dedicating the excellent Albermarle or Newtown Pippin to that hive of cloistered virtue?

"Ah! I thought it must be 1894. Thank you, I will."

Now as to climate. We can divide your country into the Grape zone and the districts north and south of it.

As a general rule Plums, Cherries and Pears all produce their best in the Grape zone. Most Apples do better north of it. We owe the peculiar excellence of our English Apples to our moist temperate climate; slow ripening is the secret as it is of good wine. Nearly all the famous vintages of Europe are grown near the northern limit of cultivation. "*Bon fruit murit tard*" is the French saying; so if you would try our Cox's Orange, Orleans Reinette and Ribston Pippin it will be above the Grape line that their merits will be best revealed.

There are some in England who say, "Why all this trouble about food and drink, ordinary food is good enough for me." I have never heard them add "Ordinary books and ordinary music." The maintenance of a critical standard is vital if we are to get the best out of our Authors, Cooks and Gardeners.

To pass through life having tasted only unripe Strawberries and synthetic wine has been the lot of many. For their salvation I have written this book.

Touched with compassion and fired by missionary zeal I send it forth into the New World, and if—

"Pardon?"

"Oh! Thank you, I will."

INTRODUCTION

Edward A. Bunyard

In the vast literature which deals with food and its appreciation I have searched for thirty years to find a precedent for a book devoted to the dessert.

The great classic authors of France have left it untouched, nor can I find in any language a treatise on this crucial subject, which may so easily make or mar a well-planned meal.

How often after a dinner ordered with intelligence, prepared with art and served with discretion, do we dwindle to a dessert unworthy of its setting. Who has not encountered the Jonathan Apple or the Jamaican Banana at a table which would scorn to provide an unacknowledged St. Julien or an invalid Port?

It seems, therefore, there may be a need for a book of the dessert such as this, but I write it under disadvantages which no gustronomic[1] scribe has faced since the time of Moses.

---

1. GUSTRONOMY, usually spelled Gastronomy—from the Greek *gaster,* a belly. As the Epicure's life is devoted to teaching this crude organ its place, and placing taste first, I suggest that gustronomy is a better word, more correct, decent, and desirable.

I have no one to copy.

In place of the wisdom of the ages I can but offer the experience of a short life, and I dedicate it in the words of Sir Hugh Plat, "To all Gentlemen, Ladies, and all others delighting in God's Vegetable Creatures."

THE ANATOMY

OF DESSERT

APPLES

No fruit is more to our English taste than the Apple. Let the Frenchman have his Pear, the Italian his Fig, the Jamaican may retain his farinaceous Banana, and the Malay his Durian, but for us the Apple.

In a careful pomological study of my fellow-men I have met but one who really disliked apples, but as he was a Scotsman born in Bavaria, educated in England, domiciled in Italy, he is quite obviously ruled out.

What fruit can compare with the Apple for its extended season, lasting from August to June, keeping alive for us in winter, in its sun-stained flush and rustic russet, the memory of golden autumnal days?

Through all the seven ages of man it finds a welcome, and we now learn that not only does it keep the doctor from our doors but ourselves from the dentists.

Is there any other edible which is at once an insurance, a pleasure, and an economy?

Before discussing the best dessert apples let us dismiss the popular error that a single test is sufficient for a fair judgement of a fruit. Often one hears the phrase, "I tasted so-and-so and did not think much of it." Flavour depends much upon the season, and many varieties require a really hot summer to develop their highest qualities. The Reinettes, such as Blenheim Orange, Cox's Orange, Orleans Reinette, and most of the russets, have their vintage years, of which 1921 will remain long in the memory. All varieties, too, have their *optimum* moment of aroma and also of acidity. A Cox's in October is a little too acid, but as the acid gradually fails, the aromatic ethers develop, and the end of November and early December see them at their height. It then slowly declines, very slowly if properly stored, and even in May, after a sunny summer, it is still worthy.

To Mr. Cox, a retired brewer, we owe this "good creature," as Mr. Saintsbury would call it, and we can picture the scene at Colnbrook Lawn, Slough, in 1825. Mrs. Cox would have drawn up her chair by the fire, the evenings are turning a little chilly, while Mr. Cox, who dines at four, is lingering over his port and dessert.

"Ah, my dear, now this is what I call a good apple. Yes, yes, very good."

"Pray, is it one of your old seedlings?" says Mrs. Cox, always a little scornful of home productions.

"On the contrary, it is one of my new ones."

"Ah well, I don't see how it can be better than a Ribston."

The firelight plays on the cut-glass decanter, and a slight reflection answers on Mr. Cox's nose, as he smiles his wise old man's smile and thinks how women are all alike—and so a great moment in history slips by.

But perhaps Mr. Cox was a bachelor....

There is in the Apple a vast range of flavours and textures, and for those who adventure in the realm of taste, a field for much hopeful voyaging.

The nomenclature of flavour is more scanty than even that of colour. How can we describe a fruit as of high flavour when this adjective by long use has gained a special significance as applied to game? All pomologists have felt this difficulty, the German with his *süsser Geschmack,* the native of France with his use of *parfumée, vineuse,* etc., and our own eighteenth-century writers whose phrase, a "delicate haut gust," though it charms the ear, conveys little to the mind. We must fall back, therefore, on the fruits themselves, and try to discern some genera of flavours, a gustatory classification.

First we must rule out the merely sweet or sour, these are not flavours though important adjuncts. Acidity for culinary fruits is of primary importance, as it is to this that their capacity for turning soft is due; those varieties which cook only to a woody texture can be brought to a normal softness by the addition of an acid such as lemon juice.

Much has been written against the "large sour apples" used generally for cooking, and varieties which "provide their own sugar" recommended in their stead. Every apple, however, is sour in its youth, and the acid gradually disappears as ripening proceeds, taking, as is natural, longer in late varieties than in the early. If, then, an apple is too sour, it merely means that it has been used too early. It is perhaps hardly necessary to point out that sourness tempered with sugar is not the same as mere lack of acidity.

In dessert apples it is noticeable that all the most esteemed sorts have a good proportion of acid, and it is the blend of this sweetness and flavour that renders them attractive, the merely "sweet" being as nauseous as in human-kind.

The right season to eat an apple is a matter of importance; to catch the volatile ethers at their maximum development, and the acids and sugars at their most grateful balance requires knowledge and experiment. Many apples will keep far beyond their period of maximum flavour, and in some this moment is so fleeting that they are hardly worth growing; a week-end away from home might prove disastrous. Times and seasons are therefore but rough guides to the correct moment; experiment alone can decide. An incontinent friend eats his Ribstons direct from the tree, and has at least convinced me that we do, in fact, place too late a season for this admirable fruit. It should be tested frequently after gathering, and will generally be found to be best used before Cox's come in in November.

In flavours we can discern a few main groups, and the early apples mostly have what has been called the Strawberry or Raspberry flavour, Worcester Pearmain, Duchess of Oldenburgh, Emperor Alexander being notable examples. The first-named fruit, however, must not be judged from barrow or shop samples, which are usually gathered far before they are ripe, and both in texture and flavour are to be passionately avoided. The really ripe Worcester has character, and, though far from the supreme heights, is in its season acceptable and the Raspberry flavour distinctive.

A second class will be the Blenheim flavour, a nutty, warm aroma which is to my taste the real apple gust; in fact, I take a Blenheim as a test case. The man who cannot appreciate a Blenheim has not come to years of gustatory discretion; he probably drinks sparkling Muscatelle. There is in this noble fruit a mellow austerity as of a great Port in its prime, a reminder of those placid Oxford meadows which gave it birth in the shadow of the great Palace of Blenheim. Like Oxford, too, it adopts a leisurely pace, refusing to be hurried to maturity or to relinquish its hold on life. An apple of the Augustan Age.

What can Cambridge put by its side? Its thin and acid airs have produced only a Histon Favourite, an apple of no period, indiscriminate and undistinguished.

The Blenheim qualities are shared by few, Orleans Reinette is its most notable analogue. Similar in appearance with an added spice as of the Ribston, this stands of all apples highest in my esteem. Much of its Blenheim nuttiness is found in Egremont Russet, while Woodstock Pippin, Ballinora, and a few others share its qualities in some degree.

A third flavour group is that of the Russets which have a peculiar "fennel" flavour; Brownlee's Russet and Reinette Grise de St.-Ogne show this in marked degree, while the French group of Fenouillets are named from this special gust.

The highly spiced flavour of Cox's Orange stands as a type, and into this group would come Ribston and Margil and a few of the Cox descendants, such as St. Everard, Houblon, and Rival. Like all classifications these divisions at once reveal their inadequacy when we consider the outsiders so far unplaced. Where shall we put James Grieve with its faint Cox flavour, Allington Pippin in whose "gelid pores" Mr. Eden Phillpotts discerned pine and grape, "the scent of quince and pear, breath of honey from the hive"?

No! Genera and classes are a vanity and can be disproved at every turn, but let them stand, critics must live.

In the matter of textures matters go more smoothly. We can well contrast the smooth, almost marrow-like flesh of James Grieve with the crisp glassiness of May Queen, which breaks with a crack as you bite it, the *cassant* or *croquant* flesh of French writers. The Russets when fully ripe are soft, as is also the Blenheim, a grain suggesting warmth, while the crisp-fleshed varieties taste distinctly colder. Cox becomes quite soft, and yet not dry, in its later stages, and those whose dental powers owe more to art than to nature, may well keep their Cox's till March. To the young, however, the crunch is the thing, a certain joy in crashing through living tissue, a memory of Neanderthal days. For them the Quarrendens and Kerry Pippins, which a far-seeing Providence has ordained to ripen in the time of summer holidays.

The need of care in selecting the right moment for each apple becomes more urgent when we consider the early varieties, where this instant of perfection has chosen to be with as great care as in the case of the more temperamental Pear. The first apples, such as Gladstone, Irish Peach, Feltham Beauty, should be eaten from the tree, or at any rate not kept over till the next day, when they will be flat and unprofitable. Of the three named, Irish Peach is to be preferred. Its fresh acidity with slight spicy aroma accords well with the warm August days. White Transparent, though usually cooked, is, at its brief moment, commendable. When ripe it becomes a transparent ivory white and the flesh is soft and yet full of juice. An acute writer has termed it a "before breakfast apple," and a tree handy to the house will not be unvisited in late July and early August. In Gladstone we have the earliest of apples in our list, quite a good *hors-d'œuvre* to the apple season, but surely never was a fruit more unsuitably named. Its shining red cheeks and impudent eye lack the dignity rightly associated with the great Liberal leader; now Gloria Mundi, with its severe angles and pallid majesty, would have some claim.

After our first early apples are over a slight pause occurs until St. Everard makes its welcome appearance at the end of August or thereabout. This is a newcomer with much of Cox in its ancestry, and its flavour is a substantial shadow before the coming event. For a limited time quite first class with much of its parental texture and juice, but unfortunately a bad grower. For the Coxomaniac this starts the apple season. At the same time comes Lady Sudeley, an apple which every garden should possess if only for its flaming scarlet fruits. The flesh is tender and melting, and at its hour of prime very highly aromatic and juicy. For the best result it should be gathered before it is willing, and stored in the fruit room for a week or two and sampled from day to day till the exact moment arrives. Grown in an unkindly soil, it can be hard and woody, and has thus lost many admirers. After Lady Sudeley comes James Grieve, in its Midlothian home a Christmas apple, but with us in the Home counties a September fruit. This is one of the very few apples resulting from the marriage of a cooking and a dessert apple which is of dessert quality. One feels that like some of the recently ennobled we know of, it is a near thing, and untoward circumstances such as a cold and sunless summer reveal the humbler origin. But given a fair chance we welcome the newcomer, thankful for the melting, almost marrowy flesh, abundant juice, and fragrant aroma.

October brings us four apples of great distinction, and with Gravenstein and Egremont Russet I should be quite content. Let us, however, add Ellison's Orange and Rival to our list.

Of Gravenstein it is hard to speak in mere prose, so distinct in flavour is it, Cox itself not standing more solitary, so full of juice and scented with the very attar of apple. This aroma comes out on the oily skin and remains on the fingers despite many washings, bringing to mind the autumnal orchard in mellow sunlight. Strange, indeed, it is that this excellent fruit, coming from Schleswig in 1760 and much grown in this country in the early half of the last century, should have been almost forgotten by gardeners.

The flesh contrives to be crisp without hardness, and it has the remarkable quality of keeping unshrivelled until Christmas and not losing flavour. I place it in this month as it is impossible to delay our enjoyment of it one moment beyond its legitimate ripeness. In parenthesis, it may also be eaten from the tree in September, but this information should be kept a close secret.

In Egremont Russet we have a fruit of superb quality, its abundant juice and remarkable nutty flavour are unapproached in their season.

In Ellison's Orange is a Cox's Orange descendant, claiming as the other parent the Calville Blanc, a marriage of the most esteemed dessert apples of England and France. It is with some misgivings that I include the result of this international union. It has, with me, a distinct aniseed flavour, and when I presented it to one educated palate with a request for a description of its flavour, I was told that he was reminded of a chemist's shop. Against this it is only fair to set the voice of a Midland connoisseur, who would select this variety were he reduced to a single apple. I therefore judge that the aniseed is a product of a warmer climate and am thankful that in a month containing Egremont Russet and Gravenstein no risks need be taken in the south.

Rival is an apple that can hardly be omitted from the collection if only on account of its beauty. A tree of this variety in full fruit, with its almost salmon-carmine tinge and light bloom, is, to an apple lover, irresistible. And why, I may ask, should we not grow fruits for their beauty? The eye requires its food no less than the stomach, and when we can combine these appeals we follow a sound instinct implanted long before modern physiologists discovered it. The brilliance of Gascoyne's Scarlet with its carmine on ivory, Peasgood's Nonesuch with its matronly form joined to the fresh colour and bloom of virginity, should decorate the dessert table even though, for interior purposes, we usually prefer them to come to us *via* the kitchen. But Rival has its fleeting moment of good flavour and can honourably figure at the dessert.

No one has a good word to say for November. The sky is "chill and drear," the leaf "red and sere," and our untethered friends leave for the Riviera to study the Mediterranean rainfall and commiserate with us on our hard fate at home. A fig for their sympathy! A month which welcomes the ripening Cox, the mellowing Comice, is a time for rejoicing. With some game in the coverts and some Burgundy in the cellar, let the population be reduced by all possible means. Let them go to lands of everlasting veal and unripened oranges, let them quaff their Chianti and other acidulous beverages; we grudge them not their fare.

November, then, is for apple lovers the Cox's month, and this fruit needs no introduction or eulogy, the Château Yquem of apples, and, to my taste, to be similarly used.

Here I shall encounter the Coxomaniacs who would, so to speak, "have it in a moog." For my part I keep it as a dessert apple, and between meals, or in the morning, choose something rather less of a sweetmeat. A little Mendelssohn goes a long way.

Early in the month we find Allington Pippin coming in season, and very delicious it is at its best. The flesh is of tender and fine grain, at first a little crisp and then becoming almost as marrowy as James Grieve, which it resembles in flavour plus a pineapple acid and a dozen fragrant suggestions of other fruits. Particular as to soil, demanding sun and open exposure, it must not be judged by the products of a dull and cold summer; the unhappy results of such seasons should pass to the kitchen, as its quince-like flavour is enhanced by cooking, and it makes a pie full of subtle memories.

Another fruit of late October and early November, the American Mother, must be included in the list, as its remarkable flavour, reminiscent of the pear drops of our youth, stands alone, and its mellow flesh at the right moment is greatly to be recommended. The flavour will not appeal to all; some I know can find no adequate words of praise, others easily come to severe condemnations. Wine merchants and booksellers, when putting forward goods which they can hardly praise fully and yet do not like to damn, call them "curious," so let Mother stand under this piquant adjective.

It is one of the few American apples of quality which thrive in this country, and one of the few that we know which are worth eating. It is evident that each nation has the fruits that it deserves, and a long period of civilisation and culture has to be passed through before Pomona considers us worthy of her higher gifts. Greece with her salted and resined wines, Rome with the pungent Garum, and pitch-preserved oysters from Britannic shores, and kindred abominations, were awarded the apples such crude tastes merited. With the finer taste born in Renaissance days, dining gradually became a fine art, and worthy palates were slowly educated. Long did Pomona hold up her sleeve the fragrant Greengage, to finally decide that under François I the moment for a just appreciation had now arrived.

And for America, in its adolescent stage, schoolboy palates were well satisfied by the Baldwins, Jonathans, Wealthys, and the like. The culture of Boston, however, insistently demanded some recognition, and so on Long Island in the early eighteenth century Newtown Pippin was "released." Alas! with us it fails to produce its subtler refinements. Can it be that we lack the Puritan austerity?

Margil is a fruit but little known, despite a long sojourn in this country, and its name provides a philological problem. Can we trace it in "marge = marle = marrow," or should we adopt the pearl origin, despite its association with margarine? Perhaps we may accept both, as its flesh is delightfully *fondant* and marrowy, and its flavour is certainly of great price. An older apple than either Cox or Ribston, it is very possible that it is among their ancestors, and it has much of their flavour, and must certainly be placed among the old masters.

King of the Pippins now comes into season, and a word must be said for this international fruit which meets one all over Northern and Central Europe. When well ripened it is very pleasant, and a slight bitter taste lurking beneath the sugar is attractive for those whose palates like a change from the more highly perfumed varieties, just as the *goût de fusil* of some wines adds to their attraction; an apple for the morning, or to clear the palate after a rather luscious sweet.

Of Ribston Pippin it does not seem necessary to write at length, as even our novelists can spell it and place it in its right season. We often hear that it is dying out or that it is not so good as it was. To the last allegation the reply is, it never was. This invaluable fruit is often starved for water and thus becomes dry and flavourless, and still more frequently is left too long in store. I may have, perhaps, assisted in this error in marking its season "till January," and now confess that I now take it earlier. Though the flesh is a trifle firm in late October the flavour is at its richest on the early side. Some of the best Ribstons I have tasted came from a tree standing by an Oxford river, in which its roots extended for some distance and thus ensured the needful water supply.

Towards the middle of this month the deepening gold proclaims the arrival of the apogee of the apple year.

In December we reach the apogee of the apple season, Cox's Orange, Margil, being at their best, and Blenheim Orange and Orleans Reinette just coming into ripeness.

I have spoken above of the great merits of the old Blenheim Orange, which a hundred years ago set a new standard of quality and which remains yet in the front rank.

Its attractions are not so obvious nor do they set out to woo a youthful love of sugar or spicy aromas, but there is a flavour which does not resemble the raspberry or strawberry, nor does it mimic the fennel, but remains the very attar of apple, unique and inimitable.

A Blenheim is one of the very few fruits which may be slightly warmed to advantage, let us say to room-temperature. There is an added richness of flavour in such fruit, and for a cold winter's evening how admirable a dessert! This, one of the best known of our apples, was raised over a hundred years ago by a cottager at Woodstock adjoining the Park at Blenheim. Little did the raiser, Mr. Kempster, think that the name of Blenheim would be known, a century hence, through his apple rather than from the great house which overshadowed the village.

Long has it seemed that, in its style, the Blenheim was unapproachable, but we have now in Orleans Reinette a fruit which is even finer. Though long grown on the Continent it is only within the last thirty years that it has become much known in England. Despite its name it seems to come from the Low Countries, where we first meet it in 1776. There is something fitting in such an origin, as it has that mellow sedateness which belongs to Flanders.

Its brown-red flush and glowing gold do very easily suggest that if Rembrandt had painted a fruit piece he would have chosen this apple. In the rich golden flesh there is a hint of the Ribston flavour, much of the Blenheim nuttiness, and an admirable balance of acidity and sweetness which combine, in my opinion, to make the best apple grown in Western Europe.

The year 1776 is significant. It was just at this time that the art of gustronomic appreciation was coming to its finest flower.

The great Carême, such worthy vessels as Grimod de la Reynière, the Marquis de Cussy, Lady Morgan, and their circle, were coming to years of culinary discretion, and the Divine Pomona decided that such single-minded devotion to art was worthy of the highest she could give. Not for the gross Trimalchio nor even for Lucullus would she dispense her highest gift. The Middle Ages with their palates ruined by Eastern spices were alike unworthy.

But when it was at last realised that the art of cookery was no longer the disguising but the revealing of native savours; when the making of wine, enriched by centuries of knowledge and tradition, approached perfection, then surely could she give of her best, happy in the knowledge that the age was ripe for higher things.

Cox's Orange and Orleans Reinette run together from December to March, queen and king of their season. Each will have their partisans, but for those who incline to the "dry" in food or drink Orleans Reinette is an apple meet for their purpose, rich and mellow, and as a background for an old port it stands solitary and unapproachable.

At this season there are many fine apples which deserve attention: Adams' Pearmain, dappled with grey spots on its red-gold sides, crisp, fresh, and sweet, a true country apple, whose origin is not, as might be supposed, from the Near East, but from our own East Anglia.

For the crunchers, whose youthful band I am still proud to join upon occasion, there is May Queen, crisp and crackling, with a savour of nuts or almost of the earth in its yellow flesh, and for those who from age or other reasons are prevented from joining us let me introduce the Cornish Gilliflower, that almost pear-shaped fruit, cinnamon gold and red without, and within a tender flesh quite suggesting the clove or Gilliflower from which it takes its name.

To Claygate Pearmain, too, must tribute be paid, a comfortable-looking fruit in sober russet with a tender granular flesh which has much of the Ribston richness, and is fully deserving a place in the best dozen dessert apples.

In February we come to the late winter apples which are so frequently spoiled for want of cultural care and from a too dry fruit store.

Too often are we reminded of those aged and wrinkled harridans who till the Continental fields with such unwearying zeal, and to those of but moderate digestive powers such leathery morsels are fraught with danger. But in a fair year we should still find our apples in March with all the plump turgescence of youth, if they have been properly handled.

King's Acre Pippin, half reinette, half russet, should now be at its best. Its chocolate brown conceals a yellow flesh which is rich and juicy, altogether a fruit of distinction.

Roundway Magnum Bonum, unpardonably omitted from the first edition of this work, must be allowed to figure here. A large green and russet fruit, faintly red streaked and in appearance far from distinguished. But under its rough exterior hides a heart of gold, a delicious aroma, and a fresh crispness which make an admirable symphony. Some enthusiasts have even awarded it first place in the Pomological hierarchy, a very pardonable enthusiasm, but with Orleans Reinette and Cox's Orange by its side most palates will place it a little lower than the angels.

As spring approaches we find the later apples mellowing to ripeness, and many of them can hold their own against the excellent fruit now coming from Australia and Tasmania, of which the

Cox's and Sturmer Pippins are often very good. Those from Tasmania especially are sometimes very close to our own growth in flavour and texture. The best way to have such fruit in good condition is to purchase a good sample as soon as it is delivered from the ship and keep it in a fruit room or cellar to ripen gradually. The warm atmosphere of a shop is not the best place for maturing fruit.

Our home-grown Sturmers are very good if thoroughly ripened, and this often means allowing them to hang till the leaves are gone. The flesh is firm and extremely juicy and of a pleasant spicy flavour, and after a warm summer we may count on them until June.

Another excellent late fruit is Rosemary Russet, an aristocrat in every way, golden yellow with a slight pink flush and flecked with a thin russet here and there. This lasts round till April and forms a useful resource at this season of scarcity.

Other good late varieties to be relied on until the Cherries come are Sanspareil, Wagener, Ontario, and Allen's Everlasting, or, as the French prefer it, Éternelle d'Allen, which sounds to us a much longer period. This last is the nearest approach we have to the famous Newtown Pippin of America in texture and flavour, and I have had it still good at the end of June, sharing dessert honours with Early Rivers Cherry.

No variety demands more careful thinning than this, an abundant crop means a total loss of quality and keeping power. The fruit then has all the appearance and texture of india-rubber, and so far from keeping the doctor at bay would invite his immediate appearance if the patient is to be saved.

Wagener, a fruit which, despite its rather Teutonic name, hails from America, is one of the best of keepers, as it has no shrivelling tendencies, and its flavour is fair, its juice abundant. Ontario, a larger less-coloured edition, keeps equally well and is quite the most handsome fruit of its season.

And so the season ends as the Strawberries begin, and our short respite from apples, two months only, is just enough to whet our appetite for the Juneatings and Gladstones of late July.

The fruits thus far enumerated should suffice to carry the apple lover through the season, but there are, of course, many which are perforce omitted.

Those who are curious in flavours should try the delicious Pitmaston Pine Apple, a remarkable blend of honey and musk. Too small for modern demands, it is worthy of a corner in any epicurean garden.

Wanstall Pippin, too, has earned the suffrages of many of the knowledgeable, a late spring fruit of most attractive flavour. Reinette de Canada, that spoilt darling of the Parisian restaurateur, is very good in March and April. We prefer it still crisp and juicy, whereas French taste waits for the *fondant* stage, which arrives later.

Charles Ross, now becoming popular, is quite good for a short period, but, like most of these half-cooker, half-desserts, the time of good flavour is fleeting.

There are many, too, who in warm spring days do not despise a cooking apple such as Newton Wonder or Lane's Prince Albert, which preserve a brisk freshness into May, and are refreshing and juicy, if not flavorous.

Of the imported apples some come into the highest rank, Newtown Pippin is supreme in its own class, the aroma of pine and the refined flavour are worthy of all praise. Of the Cox's and Sturmer's from the Antipodes we have spoken, and to these we can add Cleopatra, often called New York Pippin, as occasionally meriting attention.

The great bulk of Jonathans, Winesaps, and their kin are apples, it is admitted, and as roughage for the ever-hungry young they play a useful part, but it has not yet been my fate to find among them a fruit of quality or distinction.

Delicious is the best of the Red apples which cross the Atlantic, and this also does well in our West Country, but not elsewhere.

It is significant that the Apple has given its best to the Nordic nations, and it is among them that it is especially esteemed.

Exceptions there are, of course, but against Jargellon, King of Poland, who fled at the sight of this fruit, we may set the fact that Schiller found his best inspiration in the scent of apples.

Latin nations in general prefer the Pear, the Queen of Fruits, but to us the Apple is King.

APRICOTS

"Apricots," said the "ever-famous Dr. Muffet," "are Plums concealed beneath a Peach's coat," and of their virtues, medical and otherwise, he had much to say which was permissible in the seventeenth century but which cannot be repeated in the twentieth.

Let us pass to another epoch and to a writer who, even in his most intimate moments, always remains quotable. "The apricot, shining in a sweet brightness of golden velvet." Ruskin—of course you guessed.

There is a satisfying richness about a tree of apricots in fruit; the dark leathery leaves serve as an admirable background to the fruits. Here and there a fruit will be marked with a vinous flush and some darker freckles, indications of richness slowly maturing within. For the complete picture we need an old brick wall, mellowed by sun and rain to a rose tint, and we have a colour effect which the flower garden will not easily surpass, and the added charm of anticipation leading to that complete absorption of the subject which Samuel Butler thought to be love's highest expression. It is in this quiet carnal anticipation that much of the charm of fruit-growing rests—as we watch the slow processes of development, the fugitive flower, its hopes and fears, the slow swelling of the fruit and the dangers it runs, until we have for the survivors an almost maternal love; and at the last—how much is our enjoyment enhanced by this accumulated weight of anticipation!

There is a universe between the meal set brusquely before you and that on which thought and careful planning have been spent.

But the perfect Apricot is not easily come by; too often we find a mealy cotton-wool texture where we looked for a translucent and melting flesh.

Too much water, lack of sun and air, are two of the faults which require correction. At its best the Apricot has a certain Eastern lusciousness, a touch of the exotic which comes strangely into our homely country. In some Persian Palace whose quiet garden hears only the tinkle of a fountain it would seem to find its right setting, fitly waiting on a golden dish for some languid Sharazade. But even in the sun-warmed Midi it is not always grown to perfection, and much of the fruit which enters this country from abroad is quite unworthy. Gathered too early, they do not even look like apricots. Pale cream is their wear, in place of the wine-stained gold that they should show. Those from Angoumois are often good, and in their native country supreme. We can, however, produce as good fruit in England, given a warm wall, thoughtful culture, and a favourable season.

The apricot season is not long. From mid-July to the end of August sees its beginning and end, and the first worthy variety is the New Large Early, one of Mr. Rivers' seedlings, which seems to benefit from its native origin, as it crops more freely than most and has much of the good quality of the Angoumois, its parent. It is of good size, a little pale compared to later varieties, but of good rich flavour, with the melting flesh which is the first virtue of this fruit.

The Old Large Early which preceded this variety is also an excellent cropper and of a yellow gold, but not quite so good in flavour as its namesake. This is probably one of Major Esperen's seedlings, another debt we owe to the "Soldat Laboureur."

The early days of August introduce a wider range of varieties, and Hemskerk is among the best, not so large as many, but very rich and rather pale in colour.

Kaisha, though small, is also most excellent, and is a Syrian variety, the name being derived, I suppose, from the Turkish *caissi* = apricot. This was sent to England by Mr. Barker of Aleppo, friend and confidant of the famous Lady Hester Stanhope, who was then studying native manners and customs in that country.

Shipley is an English seedling raised at Blenheim by the then gardener's daughter, well worthy of its famous origin.

The well-known Moor Park reminds us also of another great house, to which it was brought in 1760 by Lord Anson, the victor of Finisterre. It was a stone that he brought from abroad, which was probably from the Peach Apricot, which was then arousing such astonishment in Continental gardens. This fruit has the rich gold we expect in the Apricot, the brown-red flush and translucent flesh, all of which have made it the first favourite in our gardens for a century and a half.

Another fruit with an interesting history is Breda, of Algerian origin, introduced to us in Tradescant's day, a smallish fruit by modern standards, but still good and very fruitful.

To finish the season we must select the Peach or Nancy Apricot, a fruit much like the Moor Park but later; here the quality and appearance is all we can desire, and after nearly two centuries it maintains its place as the largest apricot grown in Europe.

The peculiarly rich flavour of this delicious fruit demands some care in the selection of its accompanying wine.

Port is too stout and self-reliant, a dry sherry accords well, but best of all, I think, a rich Sauterne.

An Yquem, or, for the indigent, a Coutet or a Suduirant, makes admirable harmony. But if a gracious Titania is present to say

> *Be kind and courteous to this gentleman,*
> *Feed him with Apricocks and Dewberries,*

many would be willing, with a graceful gesture, to waive the question of wine.

CHERRIES

I have a deep compassion for our town dwellers who know so little of fruit at its best. How many of them have ever tasted a ripe cherry, one of those that we gather on a July day, so full of juice and tender of skin that it would burst at the very sight of a bushel basket? No, cherries at their best are for the garden owner—

> There cherries grow that none can buy,
> Till cherry ripe themselves do cry,

sang Campion, in reference, I admit, to another matter.

And those who can grow their own fruit are strangely lacking in enterprise in the matter of cherry varieties, and they leave to their gardeners the selection in most cases; and gardeners are perforce conservatives.

The Bigarreaux family is fairly well known and many of the soft Geans are grown and appreciated, but how rarely in England do we meet the attractive "Dukes" and the *cerises proprement dites* of France, all of which thrive so well in our climate. The Duke cherries are known in France as *Anglaises*.

The name Bigarreau is now rather shorn from its original meaning of two-coloured, red on yellow—and is applied to any cherry with firm flesh whether the flesh be "white" or black. The soft-fleshed cherries are Guignes in France and Geans in England, these again being "white" or black.

These two classes are the outstanding ones, but beside these are the Morellos, which are well known, and their name, "Little Moors," suggests a Spanish origin. Of this class there are many varieties, and they find their fitting place in the kitchen or meet a glorious death in a jar of old brandy. Not quite to be despised at dessert is the thoroughly ripe Morello; the slight astringency is to some palates attractive. The last group are the *cerises* of France or Amarelles, for which we have no English name. These are the sour cherries of a bright transparent carnelian red, sometimes known as Kentish or Flemish cherries and in America as "pie cherries."

Coming as hybrids between the above groups we have the Dukes, of which May Duke is best known. They may be either black or transparent red, probably according to whether the parent on one side was a Morello or an Amarelle, and it is in this family of Dukes that lie many greatly neglected fruits. A tender skin, which, however, does not crack like the Bigarreau under stress of weather, contains the most delicate flesh with a slight bitter tang—varying in the varieties, but always just enough to remind one of their origin—a kind of *goût de fusil*.

Let me add to my testimony the words of a learned doctor, the famous Venner of Bath, whose *Via Recta ad Vitam Longam* should be in every hand, as doubtless it was in that year of light 1637.

After some general remarks upon cherries, their effects—and after-effects—he proceeds to the Dukes: "But some are farre more wholesome than other, the best and principalest are those that are of a red colour, and of a pleasant sour-sweet taste, for they delight the pallat, excite the appetite..." but we will not follow them further; let it be enough that the end of their wanderings is to give the body "a commendable juyce."

Though my intent was to omit all recipes I must give that for a cherry pudding which may perhaps be known as "Dr. Venner's." "Cherries being boyled with butter, slices of bread and sugar, between two dishes, they delight the pallat, excite the appetite and yeeld a good and wholesome nourishment especially for hot and dry bodies." To those of my readers in like case I heartily commend so attractive a corrective.

The cherry season begins with Belle d'Orléans, usually ripening about the third week in June, its transparent amber washed with salmon pink. At the same time the first black Gean comes in bearing the name of Guigne d'Annonay and scoring one over Belle d'Orléans by its greater hardiness. It loses on size, however, to make up in crop, and our choice of the two will be governed by our garden resources.

In mid-June comes the popular Early Rivers, a large soft black fruit, sweet and very rich when well ripened, but shop samples are rarely so, as they would not then travel. To know Early Rivers, or indeed any other cherry, at its best, one must walk through the orchard a fortnight after the crop has been gathered, and here and there a fruit which has been missed will reveal to the gleaner what a cherry really may be.

For some time Early Rivers stood alone in its season as the first large tender black cherry. We have now, however, several introductions from France and Germany which come in at the same season. The Early Black of Werder indeed often comes in a few days before and is equally good in flavour and larger in size. Bigarreau Schrecken, despite its name, is really a Gean and is large and attractive with its shining black coat, but not quite of the best flavour. The same may be said of Bigarreau Jaboulay.

Towards the end of June comes May Duke, the best known of its class. Of its tender and rich flesh and faint ratafia flavour it is needless to say much; gardeners know it well, and if one cherry only can be planted, here it is. Slightly before May Duke comes the first Red Duke, Impératrice Eugénie. This is a true cerise in the French sense, tender and melting, with a nice admixture of sugar and acid, a most refreshing fruit for which I would always forsake any other cherry of its season. The rich carnelian red of the fruit makes it an object of beauty on the tree or table, and for those who like the dry or "sprightly" in food nothing can be better.

As July comes in, the cherry season begins in earnest, and so many lie before us that choice becomes difficult. There will, however, only be one opinion about Waterloo, to many the best of all cherries. A black fruit with tender flesh, extremely sweet in flavour and the faintest tinge of acid, suggests, as does its growth, that a little of the Duke blood has crept into its ancestry. Like so many superlative things it is a little niggardly in crop, but we must accept this as the way of the world.

Beside the "brune" of Waterloo let us set the "blonde" of Frogmore Early, which matches it in all points of excellence. Raised in the Royal Gardens of Windsor in 1864, it has now made its way to the front as the best early white cherry, and no gourmet's garden should be without it. Following this and almost as good is the older Elton, equally tender, but, alas! somewhat uncertain in its cropping in some places.

The Dukes now enter their main season and are all so good that it is hard to pass any of them by.

Reine Hortense, a rich carnelian red fruit, with a rather surprising yellow interior, is most delicious, and, despite its poor crop, must be grown in any collection *d'élite*. Belle de Chatenay and Belle de Choisy are both excellent in the same group and quite fair in productiveness. Royal Duke, coming about mid-July, perhaps marks the highest. It is a dark fruit, but the richness of its flesh and delicate balance of acid and sugar put it very near the first place of all cherries in my heart. To cook it were a vandalism, but should a good crop overtake the daily consumption, then a *compote* will, I fancy, prove irresistible to most sharers. There was one year when I had a plethora and some went into bottles and proved unsurpassed in flavour. The sad truth must be told: this supreme fruit crops but poorly.

The middle of July sees the first Bigarreaux of quality coming to ripeness; all the earlier varieties, it will be noted, are Geans and Dukes. Now the Bigarreaux, using the word in its sense of firm crackling flesh, are by some considered a blot on the cherry scutcheon. "Indigestible" is the word passed round, and we admit there is some truth in it. But if they are really mature, then we may qualify the damning word by "slightly."

For the young and eupeptic nothing can equal the joyous crunch of a firm Bigarreau, the next best crunch to the apple's unequalled sound, and for them we marshal the noble Emperor Napoleon, the Kent Bigarreau, Noir de Guben, Geant d'Hedelfingen, as worthy of the group.

Emperor Napoleon is quite good in flavour when really ripe, and then it should be a dark, even blackish, crimson on the sunward side, not the washed-out blush on pale yellow which its poor immaturity usually offers to townsmen.

July also brings us the noble fruits of the Gean family in Black Eagle, Black Tartarian; the first may be described as a later Waterloo, not quite so sweet but nearly attaining the supreme position.

Black Tartarian is a large corpulent fruit, bossed and uneven, and history associates it with Prince Potemkin and Catherine the Great, and for such lusty company it is in no way unfitted. The black, finger-staining, napkin-ruining juice makes it perhaps a fruit for garden strolls rather than for the decorous dessert.

As August comes in the season draws to its close, but there are still a few varieties of merit. Bigarreau Emperor Francis is an admirable fruit of a deep blood red. For the blacks, Geant d'Hedelfingen and Tradescant's Heart will satisfy all tastes, the last having a historical flavour hanging over from Elizabethan days when it first arrived at Hatfield for the great Lord Burleigh.

The Dukes make their exit with a worthy representative, Late Duke, a rich fruit with deep-red skin and a pale yellow flesh.

FIGS

The Fig, that "sweet sister of the Vine," is so closely interwoven with the history of Western Asia and Europe that we might well think that in the Mediterranean, at least, it was co-existent with our earliest civilisation.

It would seem, if our savants are right, that it was unknown to Homer, at least in the *Iliad,* and some contend that the passage which mentions it in the *Odyssey* is but a later interpolation.

We are on surer ground in the days of Plato, whose nickname, Philo-sukos, shows that he had a taste for this fruit, and we remember that Xerxes always had on his table a dish of Attic Figs to remind him of that yet unconquered country.

From that day a host of varieties streamed westward, and now each Mediterranean country has its own distinct fig flora, and even England can claim to have raised a few varieties of no small merit.

A long-suffering and hardy plant, the Fig has migrated northward, and even in our climate produces worthy fruit in favoured districts. How many of those who pass through Trafalgar Square, I wonder, notice the well-trained figs on the façade of the National Gallery?

We cannot ask the Fig, so far from its Eastern sunshine, to show us its best qualities in our climate, but there are several varieties which do good service, and if a cold greenhouse is available for their culture then a much larger range of sorts may be grown.

The earliest of the home-grown outdoor figs is the White Marseilles, a pale green fruit with a pearly opalescent flesh. This is very sweet and should be a standard variety in every garden.

Of the art and manner of eating and gathering figs much has been written. They are ready for gathering when a drop of nectar appears at the eye, and often the side splits slightly under the pressure of juice. Short of this period they will be dry, woolly and tasteless, as are so many of the imported fresh figs, gathered perforce before these crucial signs reveal themselves.

A fig should be peeled always, as there is often a slight green taste in the skin which is not palatable.

The best all-round variety for British gardens is the Brown Turkey, a medium fruit with a chocolate rather than brown skin and a deep red flesh which is of excellent flavour, sweet and rich. At the same season comes Brunswick, a large and rather gross-looking fruit formerly known as the Madonna, but upon the arrival of George I it was rechristened. It is not recorded if His Majesty accepted this as a compliment, but it has a certain Hanoverian lustiness, and so the name has remained.

Fruits of this variety often grow to a preposterous size, but they are good in a warm year, and trees are often seen in old stable yards or on farm buildings which attain a great age and seem to thrive on neglect.

Good as all these outdoor varieties are, the greenhouse will enable us to extend our season and quality and include such exquisite things as the White and Black Ischia, whose small fruits enclose a honied sweetness which no other fruit can equal in our climate. Bourjasotte Grise with its brown-red almost jelly-like flesh is in the very foremost rank of figdom, and among the sombre regiment of purple or black varieties, Negro Largo, Negronne, Violette de Bordeaux will all meet the epicure's approval.

As to the dried figs these are for youthful palates; no one who is drinking wine or dining, as do the wise, with a thought ahead for the final benediction of the cigar, could offend their palate with so pungent and cloying a sweetmeat.

Figs or dates and milk are for the Arab a meal; let us in our charity leave the dried fig to them and to those youthful stomachs in our midst to whom sugar is a stimulant. It was, I suspect, to the dried fig that Charmian referred—

O, excellent, I love a long life better than Figs.

The fresh fig met with the approval of Dr. Muffet, provided always that it was taken with wine, and they could then be relied on to "ripen a cold, cleanse your pipes, and clear your countenance and nourish more than any tree fruit whatsoever."

The essay on the Fig as an instrument of history has, I fancy, yet to be written, but material abounds. Was it not for this queen of deliquescent fruits that the French invaded Italy and so learned the art of gustronomy?

Was not Cato's sudden production of a ripe Carthaginian Fig the signal for that most bitter and relentless war?

But we, in these happier days, can grow our own figs in the shelter of our garden walls, and in August and September may sycophants, in the Greek sense, flourish and abound.

GOOSEBERRIES

The Gooseberry is an English fruit bred in this country and producing its best qualities in our climate.

It owes its development to the Midland workers who raised new seedlings for competition, whose sole test of merit was weight, and so was the Big Gooseberry born in the smoke and moisture of Macclesfield and other industrial towns. This development took place in the early days of the last century, and the names given to the new seedlings reflect the political history of that time. Before us pass the figures of Lords Brougham, Derby, and Eldon, and behind them, we regret to say, those other political hangers-on, Ranter and Bribery. Nor are the Royalties forgotten; Queen Caroline, the Prince Regent (dull claret red, very large oval), and the Princess Royal figure in our lists to this day.

The result of this great interest in the Gooseberry has been to increase its size and possibly its flavour, but best of all to combine these two qualities so that the big fruit of to-day is in many cases of excellent quality and well worthy of the gourmet's attention.

The plebeian origin of the Gooseberry has been, I fear, a handicap to its appreciation at cultured tables; it has been regarded as a fruit for children or a substitute for something better. This should not be so; the Gooseberry has a quality all its own, and a flavour which, if found in an imported tropical fruit, would be exalted in the most fervent language.

Too little are the best flavoured sorts known in our gardens, there being all the difference between the ordinary and the best that there is between the Victoria Plum and the Transparent Gage.

Let us first consider the green varieties which have, I think, the palm for flavour over the other colours, and as there are those who object to hairy fruits I will name these apart from the smooth or merely downy.

The season opens with the Early Green Hairy, sometimes known as Green Gascoigne, a very delicious fruit of middle size. This is soon followed by Glenton Green, of similar appearance and even of better flavour. Did I in a weak moment venture to select one fruit as the best flavoured of all I rather fancy it would be this on which the lot would fall.

To pass to the smooth class, the earliest is Ocean, a fine large and well-flavoured fruit whose deep sea green proclaims the appropriate naming. A small variety of the same colour and most exquisite flavour is Rosebery, named not in honour of the well-known Derby winner, but as it was found as a tender seedling beneath a rose tree, or, at least, that is what they told the children. In mid-season comes Langley Gage, a paler colour leaning more to yellow, of the highest quality, and to some the best of all gooseberries. The latest of all in this colour class is Lancer, large and well flavoured, and, despite its hundred years still growing and cropping with all the vigour of youth. As August gooseberries are in such demand when schools break up, lateness is a virtue which can hardly be overrated. No garden yet grew more gooseberries than the young people were able to deal with.

In the white group there are a few which are really a milky white, and the first of these is White Swan, large, only slightly hirsute and of rich flavour, and the same may be said of Mitre, which closely follows it. The last of this group is Snowdrop, one of the best flavoured of all.

The Smooth White begin with Careless, and then Transparent and Antagonist will see the season through with credit.

Yellow is a colour in this fruit which may vary from the true golden yellow of Early Sulphur, the first of all, to the dull olive yellows of such as Leveller or Gunner.

Of the smaller varieties, Early Sulphur, Golden Gem, and Cousen's Seedling, all hairy but the second, will satisfy the most exigent, and for the large varieties Leveller and Leader in the smooth group, and Criterion, Gunner, and Catherina will match them in the hairy yellow class. The last three will be approved by the gardener in view of the autumn show, and might, with luck, even attain the notoriety of the London press.

Red varieties are mostly of large size, but the old Ironmonger and Red Champagne, small as they are and very hairy, have a savour of their own, and should not be overlooked.

The large fruited ones worthy of dessert are Beauty (smooth) and Whinham's, perhaps the best flavoured of the reds.

It must be admitted that the red varieties cannot compare with the greens for the highest quality.

As to the time and temperature for gooseberry-eating opinions differ. A friend tells me that the moment of moments and the day of days is on the return from church at 12:30 on a warm July day when the fruit is distinctly warm.

For my part I prefer gathering while they are still cool and keeping in the fruit room till wanted. But the Gooseberry is of course the fruit *par excellence* for ambulant consumption. The freedom of the bush should be given to all visitors, as it is thus that we pass back to those days of the prime when fruit was gathered without the dark terror of the annual show hanging over us, and the exercise of gathering, too, is beneficial to the middle-aged, and also stimulates their absorptive capacity.

GRAPES

The Grape has played a part of great and perhaps of prime importance in the history of human civilisation.

Where can we find the reason for that crucial abandonment of the nomad life for the sedentary? Surely in the vegetable world. Animals, ambulant as they are, could follow the seasonal migrations, but some static reason must have presented itself, and I like to think that this may have been the vine.

We can picture the Father of our civilisation, genial and complacent amid the stir of camp-breaking, answering those who urged him to his packing, "No! I stay here until this grape juice is finished. It gets more tasty every day."

Thus was sown the seed of culture, and from that day all creative art and knowledge of nature have been the gift of the wine-drinking nations.

To us in the North the Grape is a fruit rather more than a bringer of wine, and, owing to its scarcity, we show it a reverence unknown in warmer climes. A certain aroma of opulence still clings to a fine bunch of grapes, suggesting broad acres and snugly walled gardens where the grape house is reserved for the climax of the visitor's admiration. The door, of course, is locked, and the gardener opens it with an air unattainable by any mere grower of tomatoes. A long and tedious apprenticeship is the obvious price that has been paid for such a pregnant gesture.

But even these glories are fading in these unromantic days when it is found "cheaper to buy a bunch now and then from the stores." Cheaper! The cheapest way to kill foxes is to shoot them, but still the joy of hunting lingers as does the pleasure of growing things for yourself.

But the Grape has been democratised and is now in the reach of all. Spanish Almeria has found a sturdy traveller in the Ohanez grape and, packed in cork dust, it arrives fresh and undamaged in this country. As its original name seems unknown to dealers it is well to ask for Almerias in the West End and All Marias in the East.

South Africa, too, is finding ways and means to send us excellent grapes, and the two Hanepoots, red and white, are very strongly musky and closely resembling the Muscat of Alexandria, if the white variety is not indeed identical, as some authorities decide.

For our own growing we must rely, of course, upon greenhouse culture, outdoor vines on walls being rather a gamble in our climate, though in a warm year they may attain a fair standard.

The choice of grapes in this country is unfortunately dominated by the show bench; prize-winning bunches are aimed at, and whether they are good to eat or not is usually a secondary consideration.

And so, by this curious divergence, we have missed the delicious Frontignans and Chasselas, which to my taste are worth all the Colmars or Gros Marocs and their like, but what self-respecting gardener would grow a grape which would never gain more than a third prize? By all means, let us have our Escholonian bunches to test our horticultural virtuosi, but for everyday use let Frontignans and Chasselas abound.

Our native grouping of the various classes of grapes differs from that of France. Firstly, our Sweetwaters are there called Chasselas, but as we use the name it applies to a juicy, tender-fleshed early grape without a muscat flavour. The Frontignans are known as a class in France as Chasselas Musqué; we use the word for small-berried, soft-fleshed grapes with a musk flavour. Finally, our Muscats are large-berried, firm-fleshed grapes of which that of Alexandria may serve as a type.

The Sweetwaters are the scouts of the grape season; coming early they are very welcome, but have not the quality and weight of the later arrivals.

We can well begin our season with Buckland Sweetwater, an English seedling with pale yellow-green berries, refreshing and sweet. Soon after comes the Royal Muscadine, better known perhaps as Chasselas de Fontainebleau. All travellers in France in August must have seen this very pearl of grapes, neatly packed in flat boxes, the golden yellow colour, faintly dashed with russet, which tells us at a glance how good it is, and, when well ripened, I place it far before any of our Muscats, be they ever so loaded with medals. The flesh is firm, yet far short of toughness, sweet short of sickliness, and the musky flavour not overdone. Every cool vinery should possess one at least of this superb fruit.

Of the show grapes the first arrival is Madresfield Court, a handsome fruit showing in its long berries one parent, the Muscat of Alexandria, and the softer flesh and black colour of its other, the Black Morocco. The skin is a little tough, the flavour demi-musky, the flesh demi-tender.

For those who like a more pronounced musk at this season there is Lady Hastings, perhaps the best early Muscat and quite first-rate.

The Frontignans now open their season, and among so many excellent creatures it is difficult to select. The White Frontignan, which, years ago, every vine house would shelter, is now almost forgotten, but we can hardly equal its delicious flavour, rich and musky; the flesh is moderately firm. This is said to be the informing grape of the once well-known Constantia Wine, so long eulogised by visitors to the Cape.

Early Silver is similar, but the flesh more tender and the musk less pronounced; the Primavis Frontignan, or Chasselas Musqué as it is often known, has a crisp pale yellow flesh with a marked muscat taste, one of the best of this group. The Grizzly Frontignan, so called from its curious pink-grey skin, is a great favourite with some; the late Lord Fisher went so far as to range it at the head of all grapes.

The berries are small, but are sweet, rich, and strongly musked; if allowed to shrivel a little become almost like the Muscatels of the Christmas season. This is a very old variety which was introduced to England by Sir William Temple, who thought it "the noblest of all grapes I ever ate in England," and so worthy of that garden of Epicurus of which he wrote so eloquently.

It is pleasant to think that we still have the fruit which Dorothy Osborne and Swift enjoyed at Sheen or Moor Park.

The small bunches of the Frontignans raise the question posed by Samuel Butler (the second) as to eating "upwards" or "downwards," but with a well-thinned bunch the perplexing problem should not arise.

In mid-season comes the Black Hamburgh, a grape which accommodates itself to the most varied conditions and is at home in the small lean-to house of the suburban home as well as those imposing structures which flank the garden walls of the big house. Coming from the East it seems to have advanced northward to Hamburgh and from there was imported into this country by a merchant of Rotherhithe, and the numerous synonyms it gathered during its journey's space do not permit even limited quotation.

An all-round grape, quite good when really ripened, but this so seldom happens that the average purchaser will class it as do the wine merchants the Champagne of 1925, "mediocre but useful."

The Muscat Hambro, which, by its shape, suggests a hybrid of the Black Hamburgh and the Muscat of Alexandria, is a delicate and delicious fruit, trying the gardener's skill, but one of the best of the black mid-season varieties.

As we come to the later varieties a great choice presents itself. Appley Towers, despite two unpromising parents, is excellent in the crisp-fleshed black varieties, and Lady Downes in the same group is also very good, if well ripened, but acid in unskilful hands.

Cannon Hall Muscat was raised from a seed of Muscat of Alexandria, brought from Greece by Lord Stanhope, and in the Letter Bag of Lady Spencer Stanhope we may read how a bunch was taken to Versailles and placed before the French gardeners, to their confusion and defeat. The Belgian king sent his gardener to England to learn the art of its culture, and had a house specially constructed for it at Laeken. In flavour there is not much to choose between this and the better known Muscat of Alexandria, but it still holds its place as a superb late variety.

At the end of the season comes the well-known Muscat of Alexandria, which in popular esteem still holds the premier place, the Cox of the grape world, and it deserves its reputation.

Doctors cheer their wealthy patients by allowing this fruit as a first step back to a normal diet; but are they wise? Excellent as it is in flavour, the flesh is a trifle hard and indigestible, and I should prefer, personally, to make my first step to convalescence with something of a more tender nature, one of the Frontignans, for example, but these are unknown to Bond Street and Piccadilly. How can they compare with the sedate opulence of a Muscat of Alexandria, so calmly regal in its paper-lined box, so obviously aristocratic in its well-nourished slenderness and untroubled bloom. No, we must give the palm to this fruit for appearance, and also a high place for flavour, though we may ourselves prefer simple hearts to Norman blood.

No grape has a more interesting history, and in its wanderings of many hundred years it has gathered many names, from which its resting-places can be traced with some accuracy. We may judge it to be of Eastern or African origin, as its earliest name seems to be Zibbibu, possibly from Zibbib, a cape on the North African coast. Under this Arabic name we find it in Sicily, where, perhaps, it came in Saracen days, and it is recorded in 1584. In Italy it is often known as Salamanca or Muscatello di Spagna, so it is probable the Spain of Moorish days knew it, and we do not meet with the name Alexandria until the seventeenth century, and it has been suggested that it is rather from Alessandria in Asia Minor than from the Egyptian town that it is derived. One venturesome nurseryman renamed it Muscat Escholata, after the brook Eschol, whence the record-breaking bunch of grapes was taken back to the Israelites, and from which day, I suppose, dates the lamentable idea of heavy-weight grape competitions.

There are a few grapes which the judicious will avoid—Gros Maroc, unless very well finished, and Gros Colmar—under all circumstances. Alas! that the West End should encourage such œnological travesties.

The Strawberry Grape is beloved by some, but to me the flavour suggests a cross between a Tom Cat and a Black Currant, and it is to most palates undesirable and happily rare.

If, as some think, it is of American origin, it may well explain certain recent developments in that country.

Not for such grapes did the Centaurs fight, nor for such wine did Virgil sing.

Were wine banished from our tables we should still preserve the Grape as a symbol of those great civilisations from which we spring.

MELONS

Of all the ideals which our poor humanity cherishes, the concept of the ideal Melon stands alone, for we know in our inmost souls that it will never be realised. With a peach or an apple full satisfaction is often attained, but in our search for perfection the Melon eludes us again and again!

There is but little doubt that a dark chapter in melonic history lies concealed in the mists of antiquity. I suspect a family scandal, a *tertium quid,* and, if I may so far offend the delicacy of my readers, I would hint that a vegetable marrow played the dastard part. From that day the Melon has never quite recovered its self-respect, and we ourselves are uncertain whether to treat it as a fruit or a vegetable. Those of the Marrovian school take it with pepper, and their opponents—sugar.

The Melon is widely spread over Asia and Africa from the tropical to the temperate zones, and America has also contributed to the enormous number of varieties which now exist. In all cases they come from regions of great summer heat, and to this fact some of their lack of quality in this country is of course attributable. We therefore find a variety may be good in one year and poor in another, culture and climate playing their part here as elsewhere.

The family of Melons is large, and we may divide it, as Melville did the whale, into folios, octavos, and duodecimos. Of the edible folios, the Canteloupe stands out as worthy of attention, the curious name coming from Canteluppi, a Papal villegiatura near Rome, where, it is said, this variety first arrived in Europe from Armenia in the fifteenth century.

The distinctive characteristics of this race are the rough warty surface, and the marked ribs which divide it into even sections, this suggesting to Bernardin de Saint Pierre its obvious destiny as a family fruit.

The next race, of octavo size, is that of the Netted Melon, sometimes called Muscat, Pineapple, or Persian Melon. This variety is usually grown in England, and it may have a yellow or green exterior, and a salmon, yellow, or green flesh.

The duodecimo need not detain us; the old "Queen Anne's Pocket Melon" is a representative now seldom seen, and may well be left for soured bachelors and other solitary folk.

The Canteloupes are more appreciated in France than in this country, and those which do cross the Channel usually find their way to the restaurant side-table. Of this family, the varieties d'Alger and Noir des Carmes are excellent at their best, the orange flesh of the second looking most attractive. In Paris one often meets a Canteloupe called "Prescott à Fond Blanc," or its sub-variety "Argentée." The curious name is said to be due to an Englishman who introduced it about 1800. These are not so good as the Noir des Carmes.

The octavo size—the netted melons—are, in my view, the best of all, and into this class must come those of similar size, though unreticulated, called "Sucrins" in France. They are almost exclusively grown in British gardens, and new varieties flash forth and vanish with all the fugacity of a popular novel.

I have a preference for the green-fleshed varieties such as Emerald Gem; their cool transparent jade interiors are attractive to the eye, whereas the salmon yellow of the ordinary melon is a rather meretricious colour—and there are so few good things to eat in this colour after the fishy world is left! Of these, the old Blenheim Orange is still, I think, unsurpassed, and in the white-fleshed group Hero of Lockinge maintains its premier position.

A last group, the Water Melons or Pasteques, must be briefly referred to, if only to say that they are not even a branch of the melon family, but a Citrullus. Beloved by the early Egyptians and the South American negro, and certain other races whose aim is distension not degustation, we leave them in their hands with a facile resignation.

It is easy to talk of melons, more difficult to grow them, but hardest of all to know the right moment to eat them. Scent is not an infallible guide: some good sorts are odourless before being cut open. Colour is an aid of little use when we have only one fruit before us. Looking for guidance, I turn to the *Almanach des Gourmands* to learn from that prince of gourmets, Grimod de la Reynière. Here we are—Volume III, page 67—"It is a fruit for *hors-d'œuvre,* it is never eaten at dessert in Paris"—in the provinces, of course, anything may happen. "It is rare that they are good, well perfumed and at their exact point of maturity." *Plus ça change.* "The flesh of the melon is fondant"; but the following must stand in its own language: "Fondante, humectante, et tempère les ardeurs du sang...ne convient pas aux vieillards...fait conter le..." but no more may we quote, and Reynière, coward-like, avoids the hint we are seeking!

The Melon, perhaps more than any other fruit, requires to be taken in moderation. History has been turned in its course, and dynasties hurled from their destinies, by the fatal effects of immoderate indulgence in this fruit.

Few of us could emulate Claudius Albinus with his ration of ten per diem, or even that moderate Maréchal of Belle-Isle who contented himself with three. Who can forget the sad fate of Pope Paul II, who, in 1471, died from a surfeit of melons; or that of Frederick of Germany, named the "Peaceful," whose immoderate taste for this fruit led him to an untimely tomb in 1493; and, horror upon horror's head, the terrible fact that his son, Maximilian I, impelled by the relentless laws of heredity, followed him in 1519 to the same place and for the same reason? Thus do we see how hardly may a man learn from experience other than his own.

Nectarines

The Nectarine is a smooth Peach, a Peach which has lost its *duvet* and has been known in France since the early sixteenth century under the name of Brugnon; it seems that England invented the word Nectarine about the middle of the seventeenth century. France has now adopted our word for those fruits which are free at the stone, the Brugnon now being used for such as have flesh clinging to the stone, relics of a day which should now be past.

But to the epicure is the Nectarine better than a Peach? Here we come to a question of great difficulty. One is inclined at first to say that generally the Nectarine is a more richly flavoured fruit, and yet when one tastes them side by side it is very difficult to say where the difference, if any, resides. I say at once that I prefer nectarines to peaches, but I very much doubt if, blindfolded, I could tell the difference in certain cases.

The quality of flesh is, however, different: we do not meet that smooth butter-like flesh in the Nectarine as in our best peaches; it is more fibrous and watery. Perhaps we may conclude that for texture the Peach has it and for flavour the Nectarine.

The nectarines grown in this country owe as much to the family of Mr. Thomas Rivers as do the peaches, and instead of the bird names of the peaches we get a series of English poets and scientists. Some of these have vanished from our gardens almost as completely as they have from the modern bookshelves. Where is Byron to-day, outside or in? Pitmaston Orange has played Einstein to the demoded Newton. Enough, however, are left to see us through a season from mid-July to October, and Cardinal, fittingly arrayed in scarlet, makes a first arrival in our houses in mid-July.

Before his day Early Rivers led the season, and should still be maintained as the second early fruit. The flesh of Cardinal is greenish white and Early Rivers has more of yellow in its tone, but both are of good flavour and with a refreshing acid quite welcome in July days.

In early August we come to the excellent Lord Napier, so long the earliest of nectarines, but now, owing to the introduction of those named above, taking a later place in the season. The fruit colours to a deep crimson brown, almost black in warm years, and, like all the early peaches or nectarines, the flesh is green. Yellow varieties only come later in the season.

In mid-August the season of the yellow or rather golden-fleshed nectarine begins, and their herald, Humboldt, is a worthy leader. The very deep crimson mottlings on the rich orange ground make a picture that suggests the very height of irresistibility; and the golden flesh, just touched with red at the stone, in no way belies the external aspect. Directly after this we come to the great standard fruit of the year, Elruge—owing its peculiar name, so it is said, to one Gourle, a nurseryman "between Spitalfields and Whitechapel" in the days of Charles II.

It is rather more than doubtful if the Elruge of our day is the same variety as known in Restoration days, but ours is probably better, its greenish flesh having a most delicious vinous flavour, distinct and yet hard to describe. Elruge is undoubtedly the fruit to have when one alone can be grown.

Hardwicke is a large form of Elruge, not quite so rich in flavour, I fancy, but still excellent.

Early September sees us into the full tide of yellow-fleshed fruits. Darwin, Pitmaston Orange, and Pineapple all make a strong claim for recognition; perhaps for melting flesh Pineapple may come first, but as good-looking and well-flavoured fruit it is doubtful if many could detect any difference between them.

A Syrian fruit we owe to Mr. Barker, Consul at Aleppo in Lady Hester Stanhope's day, is Stanwick, a white-fleshed fruit of a remarkably rich and vinous flavour which is known among gardeners as the Stanwick flavour.

It is a fruit of the very first quality, and if gathered a little before it is ripe, and allowed three or four days in the fruit room, during which it will shrivel a little, we may have it at its best.

The month ends with Spenser, a green-fleshed variety, and Victoria, of similar appearance, the first-named having rather better garden manners.

Both are worthy creatures and make a fitting epilogue to the three months which nectarines have consecrated with their presence.

The Peach came, as we now know, from China, but where and when it produced that happy freak, the Nectarine, we know not. If, as some have thought, inheritance is but memory, let us be thankful for that day when the downy covering of the Peach slipped her maternal memory and produced the Nectarine, one of the great triumphs of our Western civilisation.

NUTS

Science has ruined the Nut as a dessert fruit. In those careless days that were the lot of our parents, nuts came on with the port and were consumed in ignorance that six cob nuts equal half a pound of red beef, and probably the beef was taken as well. But who now can look a nut in the face when a guilty dietetic conscience tells us we have already absorbed our due quantum of protein and carbo-hydrates? The Nut, so long a matter for elegant trifling, has been turned into a diet, a food for Fabians and such unworldly breeds.

But I write this short chapter for the happy few who still pre-serve a healthy ignorance of their internal processes, to whom "in-nards is innards," to be treated rough if need be, and not allowed to dictate.

Such children of Nature still exist; and in the Commercial Room in many a country town, and in the Senior Common Room of more intellectual centres, "the wine" still finds nuts by its side on the shining mahogany.

"To hell with hydrocarbons!" runs the old-world toast.

The blending of wine and nuts has the authority and charm of antiquity. Who can forget the moving plea of Eupolis in his immortal *Taxiarchs:*

"Give me some Naxian almonds to regale and from the Naxian vines some wine to drink."

So, too, Phrynichus, Heracleon of Ephesus, and Plutarch of Chaeronea, in lines too well known to need quotation.

In this country we associate particularly the Cob and Filbert and the Walnut with wine, and they take the place which cheese occupies in France, as a background on which we can detect the subtle shades of vinous flavour.

The Filbert should be first mentioned, on the score of antiquity, and the name commemorates St. Philibert, on whose feast day the nuts become ripe. There are two varieties, the white and red, the last having a bright red skin which creates a pleasant surprise if introduced early in the evening's proceedings.

There is a pleasant sweetness about these filberts which for many centuries contented our forebears, but in the early nineteenth century we find the "Cob nut" appearing, a larger and stouter nut, and, as my philological guess, I venture to suggest it is so named for the same reason as the equine cob.

Originally the Cob was supposed to have its husk open, showing the nut within; while the Filbert has its covering quite closed, concealing the nut.

New seedlings, however, arrived with the cob-sized nut but the closed husk, and once more the system had to retire before the facts.

For the best cobs we have to thank one Webb, one of the great eccentrics in the true Waterton tradition, and, like so many cranks, he merely anticipated coming events. Smitten by an irresistible anti-alcoholic phobia, he dug a grave in his garden into which he hurled the contents of a creditable wine cellar, and then erected a monument over this incredible interment.

He then proceeded to raise seedling nuts of superb quality, and we may well imagine that their seedling roots dug deep into the soil and, maybe, drew some merit from its strange enrichment.

Some of his best, Garibaldi, Webb's Prize, and Duke of Edinburgh, serve to keep his memory fresh; and the last has, I think, the best flavour of all the cob nuts. The Cosford, coming probably from Suffolk, is also of great excellence, its thin glossy shell being distinctive and attractive.

The Kent Cob, now the most widely grown of all, was raised by a Mr. Lambert of Goudhurst, Kent, in the heart of the nut country. This is the nut which appears in Bond Street in September and the autumn months, very handsome in its russet livery, and it is of good flavour. The husk should not be removed before bringing to table, as it is a decoration, and nothing which facilitates the leisurely consumption of nuts is to be discouraged. The quiet selection, removal of the husk and leisurely handling in the crackers are nineteenth-century virtues deserving all encouragement.

WALNUT

The Walnut came to us from Roman hands, as its name *wealh* or foreign nut indicates, and its high esteem is witnessed by its name, *Jovis glans*, the nut of Jove.

From early days we trace a jovial influence, and in changing its association with Falernian to join the modern port it is but following an old tradition.

Of its more recent uses in combination with toffee and chocolate little need be said: the Augustan age knew no such illicit liaisons; to wine and wine alone it should be consecrated.

As a native of the East it lacks in this country, often enough, the days of sun which it needs to bring its fruit to perfection, but here and there we find a tree which has adapted itself to our climate, producing some not unworthy nuts. Such trees are all seedlings and therefore nameless and unobtainable in the markets in quantity, and we must therefore fall back on walnut countries, such as France, for our supplies for winter use, reserving at present our native nuts for our more immediate purposes.

Of the imported nuts which are dried by heat to ensure their keeping, the best are Mayette, Franquette, Chaberte, and Parisienne, and French authorities consider the first-named to have the best flavour.

The giant variety known as the Double Walnut or Bannut, and in France as à Bijoux, grows well in this country, and sometimes fills its gigantic shell, but more often does not.

ALMONDS

The Almond, that excellent nut now too little used in English desserts and cookery, is of foreign origin, though occasionally a home-grown tree of the sweet or white-flowered variety will set fruit, as sometimes does the pink-flowered variety, leading the suburban errand boy to bitter tragedy.

From Spain and other Mediterranean countries we are now provisioned as in the Middle Ages, when, to judge from the frequency of marchpanes (marzipan) on the festal table, vast quantities must have voyaged through the Pillars of Hercules.

The Jordan Almond is best known, and its long, smooth, mussel-like shell is distinctive. They are more largely grown around Valencia, I believe, than in Palestine.

The green almonds so favoured for dessert in France are seldom seen in this country; the favoured varieties are Princesse and Thin Shell. It is said that repeated gathering of the fruit in the green stage finally kills the tree; a curious fact, if a fact it be.

CHESTNUTS

Chestnuts are most happily met with before dessert, in my opinion; but who can quite resist them roasted in the shell around the school-room fire, or in those ambulatory stoves which winter sometimes brings forth in London and Paris?

I remember walking down the Rue de la Paix ... but, of course, in the dead season!

A thought too farinaceous for a nut, I think the Chestnut finds its best end within a bird of some sort—and preferably a dead bird. Here its soft pastiness makes an admirable ground on which more pungent flavours may display themselves, a more attractive background than the (nearly) all-conquering potato.

HICKORY OR PECAN

This is the great contribution which North America has made to our dessert.

Their Apples we can excel; Spain can hold their Oranges at bay; their Peaches are quite fortunately unexportable; but the one nut their country has originated is at its best excellent—a walnut in a torpedo, as it has been described.

At present the wild nuts predominate and are thus seedlings of varied shapes and flavours, but we shall soon have some excellent standard varieties available. Belonging to the walnut family, it has much of its character, and the flavour is very similar.

BRAZILS AND OTHER EXOTICS

The fresh Brazil, which Nature has decreed shall not be ready for the English Christmas, is a good nut and worthy of a limited attention. When, however, it has been kept for a year or so it takes an oily nature which only the most active of livers can painlessly discuss. At this stage it should be lighted with a match to amuse the children, and its yellow flame has brought many an uncle a deserved popularity.

And of the other nuts what can be said? Coco Nuts, good food for tomtits, and to enliven the Nonconformist bun.

I am informed that Monkey, Ground, or Pea Nuts are eaten in America, and certainly Film villains seem to have contracted the habit. Well-groomed heroes, I gather, abstain; and who shall grudge them their reward?

PEACHES

The eating of peaches is an art which has its technique as well as its traditions. It cannot be better exposed than in the anecdote related of Petit Radel, the eminent bibliophile and gastronome to whom was entrusted the honourable and responsible post of pregustator to his Most Christian Majesty Louis XVIII.

Seated in his library on a warm July morning, Radel had given orders that he was not to be disturbed. The discovery of an un-recorded edition had raised certain problems on which a morning might profitably be spent. It was therefore with some annoyance that he heard an approaching footstep and saw the door slowly opening. His expostulations, however, were hardly uttered as through the half-open door appeared a hand supporting a basket of peaches in all their glory of crimson velvet. Wily old Christophe! He knew that his gardener's apron could enter where others were excluded, provided that he brought with him some worthy samples of his craft.

"Enter, Christophe, enter."

The basket is placed on the table and the fruits examined from all sides. What richness of colour! What admirable *duvet*!

Then to the next step. Christophe takes out his ivory knife and divides a fruit into four parts and presents one.

"Taste the juice."

"Excellent."

A second portion is given.

"Now the flesh."

"Incomparable."

A third. "Taste the aroma."

"Unsurpassable."

The last portion is then offered with the injunction: "Taste the whole."

But the bibliophile had exhausted his adjectives. A heavenward glance filled the vacancy, and Christophe retired knowing that his peaches would reach the Royal table.

In this anecdote lies the whole technique of gustatory appreciation, as the experienced wine drinker well knows. Savour the various qualities separately, and then the symphony as a whole.

Most musicians are gourmets, and their skill in hearing the individual instrument in the orchestral combination stands them in good stead when confronted with the "dark secrets of a rich ragout," and in the Peach and Nectarine they can appreciate that delicate balance of sweet and sour and the overtones of rich aroma which give such scope for the intelligent palate.

As with all fruits of prolonged season, earliness and highest quality are rarely combined; we must wait for the full tide of mid-season, when youthful crudities are outgrown. Equally in the latter days we must not expect the richness of the prime. So in mid-July from outside walls we start our season with Amsden June and its twin sister Waterloo, and as we welcome them we do not criticise too hardly their rather watery flesh.

It is difficult to choose between the pair: both are a little apt to have their flesh clinging to the stone, and in flavour there is a very close similarity. They are welcome for their earliness, and our thanks are due to America for the introduction of a race which has enabled Europe to open its peach season two weeks earlier than before.

Immediately following comes Duke of York, an excellent early fruit of better garden behaviour than the American twins. The skin is of a rich crimson hue, and the pale greenish-yellow flesh melting and refreshing.

Hale's Early, which follows, is another American variety, and there is probably no peach more widely grown in this country. Its fertility and hardness, its placid acceptance of much cultural torture, have made it popular from the suburbs to the country cottage garden.

It can be grown to very large dimensions, but is more often seen of golf-ball size, owing to the lack of courage in thinning. The flavour of such fruits is, of course, unspeakable, and even in larger specimens a slight astringency sometimes lingers in cold seasons; nevertheless, we cannot do without Hale's as an all-round fruit.

We now come to the excellent "bird" series which provide Mr. Rivers, their raiser, so enduring a memorial.

All the fruits with bird names, Kestrel, Peregrine, Goshawk, Sea Eagle, etc., came from this source, and there are but few which do not reach the front rank.

Kestrel, a fine dark crimson fruit, comes to ripeness in early August and has a very rich flavour and much sweetness. The only fault one can reproach it with on the dessert table is a slight stringiness of flesh. Its vinous flavour reminds one that it had a nectarine for one parent.

In mid-August we have Peregrine, that finest of recent peaches, combining flavour, appearance, and good crop in a manner rarely found; and if one peach only is to be grown, this would be certainly my choice. The flesh has the firmness and finer grain of the later varieties, and the flavour is very near to the highest standard.

As the midmost days of August come round we advance into the most favoured and central season of the Peach year: from then until mid-September we touch the heights of flavour and texture.

Crimson Galande, with its dark marbled flush, is a worthy herald, and the pale flesh flecked with red at the stone, of great richness and flavour, must bring it into any representative collection. Early Grosse Mignonne at the same season is a dangerous rival, paler in colour, but in flavour and freshness almost as good; and it is hard to decide to which the palm must be given.

As August passes on we come to one of the old invincibles, Royal George—Walpole's Royal George—and, unlike him, it has won its way into the firm affection of the nation.

There is a certain Hanoverian lustiness about it—"cheeks a deep blood red," we read—and a vigorous constitution and hardy habitude made it the stand-by of many gardens.

In flavour we can find no fault, and so it takes its place to-day, as a century ago, among the indispensables.

Goshawk also comes in towards the end of August and is deservedly popular. In a sunny year its red-brown flush approaches blackness, but the flesh preserves its pale colour and has a juicy and melting quality in which sweetness, acidity, and vinous flavours blend in happy rivalry.

As the first partridge comes to table an embarrassment of riches lies before us. The vinous Violette Hative, the rich and generous Barrington, the peerless Bellegarde! How happy could we be with all. There are some, and judges of no mean capacity, who put Violette Hative at the head of all peaches; others, with whom I agree, claim that place for Bellegarde. Who shall decide between the claims of a Lafite and a Margaux? The scale is turned for me by the wonderful solidity of the Bellegarde's flesh, a solidity as of good butter, and as readily melting.

The nearest analogy in the fruit world is the flesh of Doyenné du Comice, so well compounded in its elements that knives fall through by their own weight, and teeth no sooner seize it than it is gone.

Yes, Bellegarde with its wide gamut of flavours and richnesses, and its not too solid flesh, stands unapproachable. What better end to a golden September day could be desired, as we toy with our dessert and see through the open windows a great tawny moon sailing bravely over the sleeping elms?

Towards the end of the month, Prince of Wales now reigns supreme, another of Mr. Rivers' seedlings which has gained its place by its regular bearing, good flavour and appearance.

We now come to the season of those golden-fleshed peaches which, strange to say, not only dwell in tins but also grow on trees, and are extremely good in countries of great summer heat.

Too often, with us, such varieties as Lady Palmerston and Salwey fail to reach maturity, and are thereby condemned as flavourless. Grown, however, in the Midi of France, the members of this family are delicious and deserving. We can, however, better them in our climate by the late Nectarine Peach—so called from its parent, which was a nectarine—and Walburton Admirable: both of which, on warm walls and in good seasons, are well worthy of the table of the thoughtful diner.

Of the gathering of peaches much might be said; let it suffice that they are neither pinched nor pulled off, but rather stroked off. A fond and delicate hand is applied, and a gentle rotatory movement should suffice if they are ripe. As the shoot on which they grow usually requires to be pruned off later on, I would rather take away a small piece, in the manner that grapes are cut, than suffer those tell-tale patches of brown under the skin which indicate that lust—rather than love—has directed their gathering.

Nor should the butler's fingers intervene.

A small round basket, suitable for table use, should be their resting-place when gathered, and so they should remain until they fulfil their final mission.

Mr. Saintsbury, in his *Notes on a Cellar Book,* asks what fruit goes best with wine. He rightly rejects the grape, but offers us instead a medlar—a fruit whose peculiar charms have not so far been revealed to me.

Pending enlightenment, I think the Peach is the best fruit for a natural red wine such as claret or burgundy. This liaison is consecrated by general consent in the home of gustronomy.

PEARS

I begin with a confession. After thirty years of tasting Pears I am still unfurnished with a vocabulary to describe their flavour.

I have heard it said by an Englishman that the matter is really very simple: there are but two classes of Pears—those that taste of hair-wash and those that do not. No Frenchman, in his most irreverent moment, could have so insulted the queen of fruits. The Pear must be approached, as its feminine nature indicates, with discretion and reverence; it withholds its secrets from the merely hungry. Fickle and uncertain it may too often be, concealing an inward decay by a fair and smiling cheek; but when all is said, how well are we rewarded by her gracious self at its best! Forgotten are our ardours and endurances in the soft rapture of attainment.

To appreciate the Pear we must cultivate "une vraie science gustuelle"; we must, as do those expert in wine, distinguish between the *sève* and the *vinosité*. A cultured French gourmet writes: "To savour a pear, a cultivated and exercised palate is necessary to appreciate and separate the subtle flavours." Listen to the same author upon the Pear as appreciated by the eye: "Pour ceux qui ne trouvent pas nécessairement que le blanc et le rose sont les plus belles couleurs, la poire est le plus beau des fruits. Elle possède ces teintes sourdes d'un richesse contenue, changeantes et sombres qui sont l'apanage des forêts en décomposition, de certaines fourrures et des grès des bronzes japonais." But if we hope that our author will help us in the search for the right words for describing flavours, disappointment awaits us. "Goût exquis," "ruisselant en eau," etc.: we can do as well as that in our prosaic English!

Pears, like apples, are uninteresting if merely sweet; the charm of Doyenné du Comice, no less than its opposite number, Cox's Orange, lies in a due proportion of acidity, and mere musk alone is to most palates an abomination.

The pear flavour must stand as a basis upon which may be laid the various overtones of flavour and acidity, and this basal flavour is experienced in all its simplicity in any of the early pears, such as the Chalk, Madeleine, and the like. In eating them you say, "Yes, this tastes like a pear"—and no more. The presence of acid, that oboe of the Pyrian orchestra, gives a zest and at once raises the mere Pear to a higher plane. The next addition is the musk, which Williams has in such notable quantity: a quality to be used with a sparing hand. Like the cooks who think that a sufficiency of truffle will carry any dish through, we feel that musk predominating is a facile and suspect quality; it requires great discretion in its disposal.

What are the other flavours which we can distinguish in our best pears? Some will detect an almond flavour, others a vinous quality, and I find even a "parfum excitant" in one French author. We also have the perfumes of the rose (in Thompson's Pear), a "parfum enivrant," of honey, noyau, and so on.

In the question of texture we are at once upon more certain ground. At the one extreme we have the crisp, breaking, "cassant" flesh well exemplified in that most undesirable fruit Clapp's Favourite, and at the other end the buttery flesh of Doyenné du Comice, which melts upon the palate with the facility of an ice.

As it is, in my view, the duty of an apple to be crisp and crunch-able, a pear should have such a texture as leads to silent consumption, and I therefore exclude from my pages all those notoriously crisp and glassy in flesh. Among the thousands of pears which exist it is easy to avoid those primitive varieties which have not learned the art of being fondant.

The first pear of the season is Doyenné d'Été, which ripens in July. A small fruit, Mr. Farrer would have called it "minutely wee," but for its earliness and refreshing sweetness it deserves a welcome.

At the time of its ripeness the wasps are usually in full activity, and it often develops into a struggle between them and the owner as to who shall benefit by the fruit.

After this comes the old Jargonelle in August, and the long calabash-shaped fruit is well known and has since the year 1600 been an inhabitant of French and English gardens. The flesh is tender, melting, and has a slight musk flavour, delicately balanced. At the same season Beurré Giffard ripens, but any trained eye can see that this is all wrong: the red cheek is not the healthy flush of nature nor the yellow ground without artifice—it is too obviously copied from those marble fruits which decorate alabaster bowls in Florentine shops.

Laxton's Superb will better fill the gap, and its qualities do honour to its respected parents, Williams and Beurré Superfin. Gathered before it turns yellow it is worthy of the most exalted company, full of rich juice and the generous musk of Williams, diluted with the brisk acid of its better-half.

With the coming of September the pear season begins in earnest, and to many it means "Williams" above all.

It is difficult to approach such a universal favourite in a critical mood, and the temptation to start off with the phrase, "I yield to none in my admiration," savours too much of the politician's flourish before destroying his opponent; while the word "frankly," so beloved of the journalist, casts a reflection on all statements not so labelled. To be quite brief, Williams is too musky for my taste, but its virtues of abundant juice and tenderness go far to take it into higher rank.

We may be proud of it as one of the few universal pears which are of British origin, and behind the old Church at Aldermaston, near Reading, may be seen a simple stone marking the resting-place of John Stair, "Schoolmaster of this Parish—erected by his grateful Pupils." His other memorial is the pear now known as Williams, but which in his own country is still called Stair's Pear, and since that year of its birth, 1770, it has travelled far. Arriving in London, a nurseryman, Williams, thought well to give it his own name, as did a certain Mr. Bartlett when it arrived in America. From thence it returns to us, inside or outside of tins; and from the sun-swept valleys of South Africa it comes home, changed indeed in appearance, but always with its own flavour and character. To have it in perfection, the early gathering such voyages demand is not desirable; in its own country a slight fading of the green shows it is ready for gathering, and then a week or two perhaps in the store or a cool cellar to bring it slowly to perfection. The yellow will gradually grow stronger and finally a few green dots are left, and the instant to seize is just when each dot has a faint aureole of green around it; at that moment we may give a thought to old John Stair, and join the band of his grateful pupils.

A more recent arrival, Dr. Jules Guyot, has a great resemblance to Williams and ripens much at the same time. Less musky, it has not the richness or quality and may well be left for the wayside barrow.

Two good September pears are Souvenir de Congrès and Marguerite Marillat, of similar season and not far apart in flavour; we should hardly need them both.

Sharing a rather coarse calabash shape, with cinnamon russet and red flush, the musky flavour is more pronounced in Souvenir de Congrès. Both are large and require carving as joints rather than receiving individual treatment. Marguerite often attains an obesity which verges on indecency. As an individualist, I have no leaning to communal pears.

Triomphe de Vienne (Vienne, the old rival of Lyons) is excellent at this season, of reasonable size, in flavour rich and vinous; it has many virtues and only one vice: in some years a trifle gritty—a fall from righteousness hard to forgive in these days of advanced dentistry. But I am told that pomologists of real enthusiasm find ways of surmounting such difficulties in the privacy of their gardens.

Of Beurré d'Amanlis there is not much to be said: in France it is sometimes excellent, but in most years with us it has a green vegetable taste which will rule it out from the gardens of the judicious.

In October the curve of quality rises sharply, and a month which sees such fruit as Thompson's, Beurré Superfin, and Comte de Lamy in perfection cannot be other than memorable. In France the autumnal months are recognised as marking the summit of *gourmandise*. Game, fruit, truffles are all at their best, and if the declining year is to some minds a time of melancholy, the gourmet rejoices with Jorrocks to see the dahlias fall before the early frost.

In Thompson's we have a fruit almost reaching the ideal: full of rich juice, sweet and highly perfumed, and a melting flesh almost like congealed water. It has not quite the firm buttery texture of Comice, but it is equally fondant. The only reproach we can bring is that it is almost too juicy to bite into at any decorous dinner-table; and yet, how sad to see the lost nectar when the knife is brought into play. A tender-skinned fruit this, requiring and deserving most careful handling from tree to table.

Rather earlier in the month comes Beurré Superfin, by no means overpraised in its name, as it is to many palates the best pear of all, after Comice. Mr. Blackmore, who grew pears in the intervals of writing his novels, thought it "one of the best, most beautiful and fertile of all pears," and he was no mean judge. His garden at Teddington was a trial from which few fruits emerged with a *proxime accessit.*

Again, a delicate fruit, which, like all the best pears, must not even be allowed to touch its neighbour on the fruit-room shelves.

For our third October pear, Comte de Lamy, Mr. Blackmore had no good word—"middling quality, and not worth growing." Subsequent growers do not agree, and I conclude that this delicious fruit was not happy in the Thames Valley. It is certainly one of the very best of all in the South of England, as it is in France, where it is better known as Beurré Curtet. A small fruit, a one-man pear, not particularly attractive to the eye but within a rich store of fragrance and sweetness, and eminently deserving full marks in any company.

But if Comte de Lamy, Thompson's, and Beurré Superfin are the Three Graces of October, what of the Muses?

Can we omit Beurré Hardy, so solid and masculine in its coat of russet and red, with its rosewater perfume and pink-tinged flesh, or Fondante d'Automne, more like an apple than a pear in form—but its russet skin conceals a melting flesh and an aromatic fragrance which place it quite in the first rank.

The two Louises, Louise Bonne and Marie Louise, cannot be overlooked, the last being named after that most acquiescent of Empresses, Napoleon's second wife, and, like her, it needs the support of a strong arm to stay its languishing growth. The flavour is very distinct and therefore less describable than usual; one thinks of an old Sauterne whose vinous quality is showing up more strongly against the sweetness of its youth—perhaps vinous is the word.

Louise Bonne comes from a slightly lower strata of society, the commemoration here being the raiser's wife. Properly we should call it Louise Bonne d'Avranches (not of Jersey), as there was an earlier possessor of the same name. There is a cheerful freckled cheek to this fruit, and a really country flush—eminently "du pays" compared with the aristocratic pallor of Marie Louise, but a good all-round fruit: though coming into the "hair-wash" class of the irreverent, such prominence of flavour is, however, very forgivable;

in a dull year when choicer fruits are tasteless, Louise Bonne then comes into its own.

In the long history of the Pear the year of 1849 stands alone in importance. The historian will be reminded of the annexation of the Punjab, the accession of Francis Joseph, while in that year America hailed her twelfth President in the person of Zachary Taylor.

But what are such things to us? An event of deeper import was preparing on the sunny banks of the Loire: a pear seed had germinated some few years before and in the spring of 1849 opened its first blossoms to the April sky.

The fruit grew slowly to maturity and eager pomologues watched its green fade to yellow, waiting for the moment of "degustation." Happy those who were present when Doyenné du Comice first gave up its luscious juice to man. Whom could they envy at that moment? Certainly not Zachary Taylor. Here at last was the ideal realised, that perfect combination of flavour, aroma, and texture of which man had long dreamed.

Two thousand years of Pear history was necessary to educate a public worthy of such refined delight, and the world's great gourmets had died still unacquainted with the perfect Pear.

How then shall we attempt to paint its charms in our chilly and reluctant prose? Let us see what experts have attained in this quest.

Let France lead, as a mother's privilege. "Chair très fine, fondante ou ferme, blanche, très juteuse, eau sucrée, légèrement astringente ou acidulée, parfumée."

Here the note of scientific aridity is surely too pronounced. "Astringente ou acidulée!"

Perhaps the phlegmatic Nordic can do better than this—let us cross the Rhine.

"Vereins Dechantsbirn. Fleisch, gelblich weiss, fein, saftreich schmelzend, von angenehmem, süssem, gewurzhaftem Geschmacke."

This has the connoisseur's note more strongly emphasised and the building up of the final climax betrays the artist, but even here we feel a lack of colour, a certain boreal chill.

We go southward. "La polpa gialla, verdastra e fina, fondente, molto succosa; e molto bene profumata, squisitissima."

Here at last is the lyrical touch, the warmth and colour we are seeking. "Molto bene profumata!" Excellent.

We cannot hope to better this in our own language, and perhaps it is not necessary, as who does not know the melting Comice, now available so large a part of the year, thanks to the Panama Canal and our own Dominions? But welcome as these sea-borne visitors are, they cannot rival our home-grown fruit after a good season. Gathered, perforce, before they are ready, and checked in their natural ripening by the necessary cold storage, they are not more than welcome understudies.

The storing and treatment of Comice in the fruit-room needs the greatest care: the fruits should not even touch, much less should they be piled. The temperature of a cellar is about right for them. When the green colour begins to change to yellow the moment of watchfulness arises, and when the whole fruit is of an even yellow the moment has arrived. As not all the fruits will arrive at this point simultaneously, great care is necessary, and no day should pass without inspection, but not handling. Some authorities recommend that at this moment the fruit should be placed in a decidedly colder atmosphere for forty-eight hours and then brought back to the fruit-room to regain its previous temperature.

As to the correct temperature for eating, opinions will differ. I greatly dislike pears at room temperature, or, indeed, nearly all other fruit. Fruit which has stood in a warm room the whole day is not at its best; I prefer to bring pears up an hour or two before use, so that they have some of the chill of the fruit-room in them, but this is a matter of personal taste; too cold—means a loss of flavour; too warm—leaves out the cardinal virtue of a fruit, its refreshing character.

But the ways of man and his palate are beyond understanding. In a Piccadilly grocer's window I have seen pears bottled in crème de menthe!

It might be feared that after Comice the rest of the pear season would be but an epilogue, but fortunately the months from December to March have much of value and interest to offer, and many superb fruits delay their ripening until this time.

In Glou Morceau we have a fruit worthy of its name, the first part of which comes from a Flemish word *golou,* meaning delicious. The smooth green skin has the unmistakable look of quality, and as it fades to a pale yellow it comes to a slow and prolonged maturity. This virtue of slow ripening is valuable, and after a warm summer we may have this fruit in good form for two months or even more.

The firm but melting flesh comes but little behind Comice in this respect, and the flavour is of the best.

Like all late pears, a warm and sunny position must be given it in the garden.

Beurré Six comes in at the same season and is very nearly a Glou Morceau in all points, but its greater hardiness makes it desirable. It is, however, ready while still green; indeed, it changes colour very little and must be watched carefully in November and December or its grass-green colour may deceive the unwary into losing its best period. So many virtues are enshrined in this fruit, good flavour, hardiness, excellent crop, that I wonder it has not been earlier known in this country.

Le Lectier, a "large paper" edition of Beurré Six, is a descendant of Williams and an established favourite; for the lovers of musk it will appeal, perhaps, more than its predecessor.

Beurré de Jonghe comes in during December and January and is of a more rustic appearance, having some considerable patches of russet. In flavour it is quite first-class, having much of the delicate vinosity of Marie Louise, and altogether it is quite worthy of the most distinguished gathering.

In January we welcome Duchesse de Bordeaux as a fruit of the very first order, and usually known in France as Beurré Perrault. It is one of the few round pears, and has rather the look of a russet apple; once through the skin, however, we find all the tender femininities we ask from the Pear: the white flesh melts at a touch and yields a fragrant sweet juice which is the perfection of balance and free from the grittiness which makes some pears so discomfortable.

Winter Nelis comes in season in December and often lasts until February, and forms a formidable rival to its contemporaries.

It is now well known to all fruit-lovers, as it reaches our markets from the Cape in large numbers, enlarged out of all knowledge by the Southern sun, but still good in spite of its too early gathering and cold storing.

As ripened at home it is rich and vinous, while the flesh is buttery and fondant. It matures slowly and so provides a resource for two months or more.

With it comes Joséphine de Malines, a smooth, green, small fruit, but so hardy and fruitful that one is tempted to give it first place among all winter pears. The flesh is of a curious rose-yellow tinge, rather rare among pears, and it has a tinge of rose-perfume in its rich flavour. In size it is rather small, but its generous crop is often to blame for this, as the British gardener is usually reluctant to thin severely, or even at all.

The above-named fruits will carry us through till March, but for those who like variety we may add a few others.

Admiral Gervais, not much known as yet in this country, is an admirable fruit of excellent garden habits and of good dessert qualities. Bergamotte Esperen, an uncouth and rugged peg-top in appearance, conceals an excellent interior, and keeps up the season till April. The flavour is rather of the pronounced order—highly aromatic, is perhaps the word—and remarkable sweetness attends it after a warm season. Those whose lodging is on the cold clay had better avoid it. Though the rough skin and general appearance of hardiness would lead to the conclusion that this fruit can be handled like a potato, it is far from being so. It is, in fact, a specially tender-skinned fruit, and if two are allowed even to touch on the shelves a black mark will appear which spoils the flavour in a marked way. Handle, therefore, as it were the tender Peach.

Another February to March pear I find it hard to exclude, the Nec Plus Meuris. It is certainly small, but so good that one forgets all but the flavour.

To carry us to the end of the season three candidates appear whose claims cannot be disregarded. Easter Beurré first saw the light in the Capuchin monastery at Louvain, somewhere about the middle of the eighteenth century, and is better known in France as Doyenné d'Hiver. In favourable years, and on warm soils, we can confidently rely on this noble fruit for our latest variety. The flesh has all those butter-like qualities we ask for, and the flavour is excellent, a blend of musk and vinous quality.

In Olivier de Serres, a name which commemorates the Father of French Agriculture, who laid out the first experimental farm in 1600, we have an apple-shaped pear, roughly russeted, and with a flavour which makes a worthy epilogue to the pear season.

Passe-Crassane is similar and well known to all who frequent Paris restaurants in the spring. It, alas! requires more sun than we can usually provide it, and must be regarded as a gambler's fruit; but most gardeners like a little flutter now and then—who has not seen the gambler's garden full of tender things which you know, and he knows, will go under at the first severe winter? Did Nietzsche plant his garden so dangerously, I wonder?

As I go back over this list, I see that pale spectres of forgotten fruits will haunt my dreams for many years. How can I defend my omissions? Where is the honeyed Seckle so dear to Walt Whitman, the faithful Belle Julie so neatly clad in cinnamon russet, Le Brun looking like a cucumber but tasting like a Williams, President Barabe among the latest, and Nouvelle Fulvie?—all these and many more are unpardonably omitted. But my readers will have the joy of finding them out for themselves, while for me remains the fate of all presumptuous selectors.

PLUMS

"All plums," said Nicholas Culpeper, "are under Venus, and are like women—some better and some worse."

The pregnant words of the Herbalist remain true to this day—so far as plums are concerned—and from the great number of varieties, which even in Pliny's days was remarkable—*ingens turba prunorum*—we must attempt to range a gathering of worthy representatives.

In no fruit, except the Cherry, do the shops treat us so scurvily: Greengages from Southern countries, usually as hard as golf-balls, and orchard-grown specimens, small, unripe, and stony, are the best we can find; the result is that the poor townsman usually considers Victoria the best plum, and it is usually the best he can procure. The choice gages are known to garden-owners only, and not all of these realise the length of season and wealth of flavour which is at their disposal.

The distinction between a "Gage" and a plum is only British, and arose from the fact that a greengage, known in France as Reine Claude, was imported by a member of the Gage family, and, owing to a lost label, was renamed in honour of its introducer. Generally a plum with a good flavour is called a gage in this country, and our selection will be mainly confined to this group; the Victorias and their like may well remain in the kitchen, very welcome when cooked, but hardly up to the best standard of the dessert.

In August we may expect the season to open with Oullin's Gage, a large, round, creamy yellow fruit of merit, firm as to flesh, and fair—only fair—in flavour, except in a hot, dry summer, when it imagines itself at home in the "Midi" climate and answers with a rich sweetness not usually given us in our average year. In dull years its destiny is the bottle, whence it comes excellently in winter months with a firm yellow transparent flesh and a faint ratafia flavour.

The early August days see the ripening of the Early Transparent Gage, that worthy descendant of the Old Transparent Gage, the King of all Plums, whose royal potency has descended in no small degree to his offspring. The Early Transparent may be quite large, but if overcropped is small and flavourless. Its great fertility has caused it to be placed rather below its merits in many hands, as no fruit more than the Plum depends on its best flavour for a judicious thinning. At its best this earliest member of its family is first-rate and has the true "gage" consistency with the richness which this family alone provides.

In mid-August comes Denniston's Superb, an excellent fruit which we owe to America, and it now approaches its centenary and retains its merits unimpaired. An oval fruit, inclining to a certain rotundity, its yellow skin is washed with pale green stripes, as if painted on with a light water-colour wash. The transparent flesh is of an admirable texture, firm but not tough, and its flavour irre-proachable. A little later we may find Golden Esperen ripening its golden fruit and blushing slightly under the sun. Here is a real sweetmeat, a *bonne bouche* for any August dinner, and a pleasing re-minder of Major Esperen, one of Napoleon's generals, who devoted his latter years to the raising of fruits at Malines. His name is better remembered as the raiser of the pear, Bergamotte Esperen. Both are worthy.

With the last days of August comes the Queen of Plums, the Greengage, a variety which is quite probably a wild Caucasian species which has wandered (as so many fruits) to us through Italy. In France it is always known as Reine Claude, and the legend runs that it is thus named after the wife of François I.

Whether the Greengage of to-day is that of the sixteenth century no one can say, and as this fruit comes very nearly true from seed there are several pretenders to the throne.

The memories of the "Old" Greengage are often a careless rapture which is hard to recapture, and there are some who think that the modern fruit is not of the Royal line. There are so many factors which influence flavour; over-cropping, exposure, soil, manure, and the age of the tree being a few; but I think that there is no doubt that we are growing the fruit of a century ago, and at its best it is so good that it is hard to imagine the supposed deterioration. In no fruit is supreme ripeness more necessary; a slight shrivelling around the stalk, a deepening of the claret dots, indicate that the moment has arrived. Alas! the wasps are not often so patient.

If we may call this the Queen of Gages—what of the King? Appropriately enough at the same season comes the incomparable Transparent Gage, often called the "Old" to distinguish it from its worthy sons. If there is a better gage than this, I know it not, and certainly there is none more beautiful. Its French name, Reine Claude Diaphane, exactly describes its clear, transparent look; a slight flush of red and then one looks into the depths of transparent amber as one looks into an opal, uncertain how far the eye can penetrate.

The flesh is firm, short of toughness, and in it are blended all the flavours that a plum can give in generous measure. Larger than a greengage, suffering less from a sunless summer, with a more robust constitution, well may we call this the King of Gages. *Ave Imperator!*

In early September we welcome Jefferson, another emigrant from America, a President among Kings, and with the characteristic Jeffersonian tenacity. It hangs long on the tree without losing its flavour, and is apt to be a little tough in fibre, a virtue in Presidents and quite pardonable when accompanied with real merit.

In Bryanston a famous English house is celebrated, where in 1831 this excellent late greengage was raised. In outward respects it is a folio edition of its parent the Old Greengage, larger, more flattened at the poles—in fact, the "oblate spheroid" of our early geographies. The flavour quite equals the Greengage, and though nearly a century has passed it is yet too little known.

Identical in season is the Reine Claude de Bavay, another seedling of Major Esperen's, a more oval fruit and of a decided yellow green. The flavour is very nearly of Greengage standard, and as it has all the garden virtues, including that of self-fertility, it is indispensable in a well-ordered collection.

At the end of September we welcome Coe's Golden Drop, its pear-like shape and champagne-bottle shoulders distinguishing it from most other plums. At its best it is a dull yellow green with strong frecklings of crimson, and at its ripest it is drunk rather than eaten; the skin is rather tough, but between this and the stone floats an ineffable nectar. The stone and rather fibrous flesh may well be discarded with the skin, and, digestion unimpaired, we come to our port in beatific mood. Should it be port, I wonder? Perhaps rather a glass of Yquem is the benediction a supreme gage requires.

As October draws near we realise that the reign of the Transparent Gage dynasty is not yet over. First comes the Late Transparent, worthy son of a distinguished father. The family likeness is obvious, and within are qualities hardly less similar.

Golden Transparent has the gracious richness of harvest under its golden coat, and the plum season ends on a note of deep satisfaction.

On looking through the varieties chosen, I see they are all green or yellow. Is there, then, nothing encased in red, black, or blue which is worthy of the connoisseur's notice? The truth is that there are very few and none of the highest standard. Kirke's in mid-September is a worthy fruit, but, while the Transparent Gage is ripe, who would prefer it? The same may be said for Comte d'Althan's Gage, good as it is; its handsome appearance and fine flavour are meritorious, but not quite supreme. Victoria—that almost national emblem, one of the many good things which have come out of Sussex—where can we place it in early September when the Greengage, Transparent Gage, and Bryanston are dominating the dessert?

For hungry holiday-makers fresh from school, for Bands of Hope, gatherings of the Faithful, and other charitable occasions, Victoria finds a welcome "in the raw"; but at home—to the kitchen with it.

There are, of course, a few byways of the plum world in which we may saunter. In early August the variety known as Stint is welcome, the best flavoured of its season, and its pale pink, or rather *œil de perdrix,* colour is attractive as is its golden flesh.

The prolific Czar, usually sold when half ripe, is quite acceptable from a warm wall in an afternoon's saunter round the garden.

There are, of course, many such fruits which, eaten *al fresco* and in a careless outdoor mood, are gratifying, and not to be despised even by the epicure. Under severe post-prandial criticism they would be justly spurned, but under the all-tolerating sky they may come to an uncensured appreciation.

The delicious Mirabelle (not to be confounded with the Myrobalan, quite another family of plums) is, of course, destined for jam, but a fruit or two fallen on the grass from sheer repletion of sweetness will not be out of harmony with that reflective stroll round the garden, for which the interval between tea and dinner seems so happily to have been designed.

There are some interiors so delicately balanced that the Plum is to them a source of inquietude and regret, though I doubt if it is always so culpable as it is supposed.

Perhaps one reason may be the ferments which reside on the skin of every fruit as it ripens, waiting for the moment when it is their proud duty to turn the sugar within to the alcohol of man's desire. These ferments may be unwelcome intruders into that mysterious warfare of bacilli and phagocytes which rages unseen in us all. Rightly or wrongly, I fancy the peeling of plums is advisable, and pass on this valuable hint to all who fear or suffer.

Raspberries and Other Small Fruits

Raspberries have long been esteemed as a dessert fruit, and did not Dr. Venner, that great citizen of Bath, commend them for "weak and queasie stomachs," as well as for many other reasons?

The raspberry of his day was a pigmy to our modern fruits, but we have happily preserved the true flavour in the giants of to-day, and in such cases size is a gain.

Why raspberries are not as popular as strawberries with cream it is hard to discover. The Framboise Melba is merely waiting to throw a double honour on its inventor and its patron.

It would, I think, be simple: cream and sugar with some faint breath of a liqueur to which my imagination will not carry me, but which will doubtless be reached in a sudden flash as soon as these words are irretrievably printed.

In the interim I find the smallest drop of a *fine champagne* in the simple mixture is acceptable to many.

The varieties which are dessert-worthy are not many, and if we have Red Cross, Lloyd George, and Royal, we can rely upon an extended season and good flavour.

The white varieties are to be recommended for their delicate flavour, and of these the old Yellow Antwerp remains unbeaten; while, for autumn use, Surprise d'Automne will, in a warm autumn, produce excellent fruit in September and October.

—

Of Currants, red and white, there is not much to say from our point of view, but their decorative value is great, and a dish of either in the lamplight is a temptation to an elegant trifling by a dainty hand which should justify their presence.

—

Of the great army of Berries, black, red, and otherwise, none come to a dessert standard; Loganberries can go to the nursery and Blackberries to the kitchen.

The British Blackberry is a fruit for out-of-doors; the American varieties for cooking purposes only.

—

The Mulberry is often delicious, and it is said that to this fruit we owe the invention of forks and all that has meant to the art of the table. Here again we feel the need of the great artist's hand to lift the Mulberry into a higher place.

—

Medlars require reverential consideration, after Mr. Saintsbury's declaration that they are the ideal fruit to join with wine. Each of us has some blind spots in our make-up, and it may be that a liking for Dickens and Medlars are in some strange way connected, as these are the only two things in which I cannot follow the author of the *Cellar Book* with reverence and gratitude.

STRAWBERRIES

The Strawberry receives as warm a welcome in June as does the primrose of spring, and for the same reason.

After several months of exotic fruits the simple freshness of the native Strawberry is as welcome to the countryman as to the jaded palates of Londoners bracing themselves for the last efforts of the season.

But the townsman knows the Strawberry at its best as little as he realises the surpassing flavour of the freshly gathered pea or asparagus.

It is said that a wealthy bourgeois of Mayfair sends a car to his country seat each evening to bring these delicacies fresh to his table, in their season; but less moneyed mortals must have a berry that is unripe enough to travel to market uninjured. Even the favoured owner of a garden often has his fruit gathered far too unripe. Why is it that the small fruit found after the main crop is gathered are so delicious and so far above the first berries which came to dessert? Simply that the later fruit was really mature. "All is not ripe that reddens" should be a text for every gardener's bedside.

Much of the bitterness felt by the rheumatic towards this engaging fruit is due to the lamentable incontinence of gardeners.

The Strawberry of to-day is the result of a fusion of the blood of the Virginian species and its South American relation from Chile. Long as our wild European variety has been grown in gardens it has not apparently played any part in the development of the modern fruit. The wedding ceremony of the American immigrants was celebrated in England, and for some years the large modern fruits were called "English" in Continental countries. Of the great number of varieties which were raised during the past century some still remain in the first rank to-day, but too many varieties have not this fixed and resting quality, and come into prominence and fade away before they are hardly known. In a list of tried favourites we find that there are many of these sturdy relics of Victorian days still overtopping the moderns. Can we, for instance, better Black Prince, that small but solid fruit, of a rich burgundy colour and notable still for its earliness and delicious flavour? This variety dates back to 1837, that pregnant date which is considered, outside of Chelsea, to have ushered in a period of unexampled development.

Only three years later came British Queen, which remains in the forefront for richness of flavour. This variety does not turn so dark a colour as some, and the flesh within is pale.

Another of the great Victorians, Sir Joseph Paxton, lent his name to an excellent fruit which still very largely provisions the markets on account of its habit of colouring before it is ripe, and thus providing a good "traveller." As often sold, light orange scarlet one side and greenish white on the other, it should be a scheduled poison, but when fully ripe and almost of a mulberry tinge, how excellent it can be. This, coupled with its vigour and productivity, makes it one to be grown in every good collection.

Another Royalty in Royal Sovereign came towards the end of the Victorian era, and this has for forty years taken the first place.

We cannot place it quite among the best for flavour, but well finished it is well worthy of any table, and possesses the great Victorian virtue of fertility.

Dr. Hogg is one of the best flavoured of all strawberries, and would it but grow it would be found in every garden. Its inveterate habit of becoming beautifully less will daunt all but the most determined epicure.

There are other main season varieties of good flavour, such as Vicomtesse de Thury (also excellent for jam) and President, pale in colour but with much of the rich "pine" flavour so desirable in the Strawberry.

For the latest we can choose between Givon's Prolific, a majestic red, and Waterloo, more than majestic—even corpulent, with a port-wine colour without and deep blood red within, rather too carnal in appearance for vegetarians, but of very rich and mellow flavour.

As a contrast come the white or pink varieties, Louis Gauthier, large, pulpy, and succulent, but almost justifying its rather watery flesh by a strong pine flavour.

The old White Pine, too, is remarkable for this quality, and both of these whites make good jam if a tawny brown colour is not despised; for the rich red colour we must use Black Prince or the Little Scarlet.

The flavour of the old Hautbois is liked by some, and the dark mulberry-coloured fruit is more curious than beautiful. To my taste it is a little too reminiscent of a raspberry a little past its best. The Royal Hautbois, a larger form of the wild species, is usually preferred.

The Alpine Strawberry is no less happy in British gardens than its Alpine relations upon the rock garden, but they are now seldom seen, another victim to the craze for size.

They are, however, one of the best of all fruits, and in August and

September become a valuable resource. The small wild variety has given certain rather larger fruited forms such as Belle de Meaux, Alpine Improved, and also a few white forms, all of which are good and have much of the true Alpine flavour, but it is, I fancy, at its best in the parent. It may be mentioned that a handful of these Alpines noticeably enrich the flavour of jam made from the usual garden varieties. Used alone, the jam is too hard and mealy, and the seeds too close together for comfort.

The Strawberry is not everyone's fruit. To some it brings a sudden rash, and to others twinges of rheumatism. This fact must be admitted and faced.

To sufferers from the second I would ask first if the strawberries they try are really ripe? And if the answer is yes—then I would advise a trial of the old small fruited varieties such as Black Prince and, above all, the Alpines, which in my own case have no ill effect, whereas the large fruited sorts must be approached with frugality and discretion.

How seldom, in this country, are we offered wine and sugar with our strawberries, in the French manner, dipped from a wine-glass with a spoon. A light claret, or Beaujolais, blends admirably with the strawberry flavour.

While there are, as we know, certain sufferers from fragariaphobia, it is happily a rare disease, and strawberries were formerly considered to have very considerable medical value.

An old writer extols them as "a surprising remedy for the jaundice of children, and particularly helping the liver of pot companions, wetters and drammers."

While too late, I fear, for most of us to experiment with the first-named malady, some of my readers may welcome the valuable hint in the last paragraph.

As to the time for eating strawberries, the Middle Ages were unanimous in banishing it from supper and late meals.

Bewar at eve of crayme of cowe, and also of the goote
Because it is too late
Of strawberries and hurtilberrie with the cold joncate.

How well we know that cold joncate!

But this way lies hypochondria; rather should we emulate Mme du Deffand, of whom Horace Walpole wrote: "She has been so ill, that on the day she was seized I thought she could not last till night. Her Herculean weakness, which could not resist strawberries and cream after supper, has surmounted all the *ups* and *downs* which followed her excess." Oh! admirable octogenarian.

A FEW NOTES
ON
WINE

THE SYMPHONY OF WINE

In praise of Wine many eloquent pens have run their course, and to those acquainted with this literature there seems little that can profitably be added.

These classics are, nevertheless, a little remote; they speak of the great peaks and summits, an air too rarefied for most of us. The glorious vintages of 1878 we may worship from afar, but what we should like to know is how can we attain the lower slopes, how far five shillings will take us in the delectable country of Bordeaux. These few notes are, therefore, for those whose ambitions are as modest as their purses.

Firstly, let me assure all aspiring explorers that all wise wine merchants welcome them. If your small orders for the cheaper vintages has a chilly reception, you have quite obviously chosen an unwise vendor. Change him forthwith. The highbrow merchant, or vinous snob, should have no place in the fraternity of Epicures. Could we all afford the *premiers crus* there would not be enough to go round.

———

In all arts the first step is to know what to look for. What are the characters of a good wine?

Perhaps they may be best illustrated by an analogy, a musical one.

The Soul of Music is rhythm, the primitive drum which answers and stimulates our heartbeats. To this is later added the sound of the pipe, introducing us to melody, and with more pipes comes harmony. When to the primitive piping we add a string or brass instrument tone contrast is born, and so on till the rich complexity of the modern orchestra is reached.

Now Wine can be considered as a symphony, and on the just balance of its components its merits depend.

Firstly, then, is the flavour of the grape, the vinous taste in its purity, which we may compare to the string basis of the orchestra; alone it would be flat, but enlivened by the acid piccolo, preserved by the light astringency of clarinets and bassoons, it comes to life as a pleasant and refreshing drink.

An orchestra, however, without brass would lack some colour, and a wine without alcohol no less so. We add, therefore, alcohol to our vinous symphony and at once place it in a new category.

There are, of course, some who like a brass band above all music, equally there are those who like alcohol as neat as they can get it. These take to Cocktails whose appeal is that of brazen trumpets loudly overblown.

To the real lover of Wine, as that of music, these fiery tones must be used with the greatest discretion. Not for them the crude assault, but the quiet and slow progression "by littles and wees" to that state of mellow feeling where charity has her favoured dwelling.

Wine is, therefore, a symphony, an orchestra of many tones and rhythms, and equally there are orchestras of many sizes. There is the imperial majesty of Burgundy, so richly scored, contrasting with the clean simplicity of an Anjou wine, a string quartet in comparison.

MATURITY

Wine is like fruit in that it is at first unripe and has then to many the unpleasant consequences that green apples are noted for. The question of ripeness is all, and hence the most important thing upon a bottle of wine is not the name, but the date. The vendor will always give you the year of his wine, if it is mentionable; if it is absent, one may assume he has either forgotten it or would wish to do so.

Young wine, like the young apple, is too acid, and thousands have been driven to whisky because "red wine does not suit them." Raw wine does not suit them, is the necessary amendment. By a happy provision red wine carries its age in its looks: young red wine is pinkish-purple, Condy's Fluid matches it nearly; old wine loses the pink and becomes clear red and fades to a tawny red.

A few shillings spent at a restaurant in learning this most valuable of all tinctorial lessons will never be regretted. Decide on your red wine of a reasonable maturity and purchase at the same time a bottle of undated "St.-Émilion," "Good Dinner Claret," or whatever figures at the cheapest end of the list. Pour out a glass of each and compare the colours carefully and then hand the undated wine to the *maître d'hôtel* with your compliments.

The next lesson is that of smell, a lesson which English wine glasses seldom allow one to enjoy to the full.

Half the enjoyment of wine is from the nose, which warns the palate of what is coming and stimulates it to an enlivened appreciation. The glass must, therefore, allow room for the nose and must be of a shape that permits the swilling round of the wine which enables it to exhale its aromas. The shape should be that of an egg after a generous decapitation, and, unfortunately, it is difficult to find in England where cut-glass horrors of triangular shape are favoured by makers. These are quite hopeless; one cannot swill the wine without spilling it, or warm it up with the hand as is often so necessary with red wines.

The only places I have found a really good claret glass are at the dealers who supply London hotels and restaurants.

Most important of all, the glass must be clear so as to show the colour of the wine. Green may be all very well for white wines so that the slight sediment, as in Sauternes, may not be visible; but red, or pink, are relics of the worst of Victorian taste and may be left to those who revel with Wallaboola Burgundies and Medicinated "Ports."

TEMPERATURE

This is the rock on which many fine bottles have foundered; it is hard to keep back the tears from one's eyes when a fine red wine comes to table steaming from the fire or with the cellar chill still upon it. No red wine reveals its qualities when cold. The delicate and volatile ethers which give aroma are not evaporated, and therefore unperceived by the nose and palate. There is one way, and only one way, to have red wine at the proper temperature, and that is to bring it into a room of comfortable temperature for some hours before the meal.

Never should it be plunged in hot water or join the cat before the fire. When the waiter says "Shall I take the chill off?" let your "NO" sound forth as a thunder-clap.

If the wine has not been gradually warmed before it is poured, it must be warmed by the hands of the drinker, lovingly clasping the wine glass, making love, as it were, to the reluctant nymph. And here comes the justification of the thin glass: Could you, Sir, or you, Madam, make love to anyone in cut-glass pyjamas?

The right temperature is when the wine feels comfortable to the hand. If it chills the encircling fingers or numbs them, it is too cold. Wait a while and play with it till it warms up to the point of revealing its fragrance. Here, again, is emphasised the need for the half-filled glass, a third-filled is even better.

White wines are nearly all served cold, as they show their characters better in this way; the brass of the alcohol is subdued to the advantage of the more delicate tone colours of the symphony. It can, however, easily be too cold; a few degrees below room temperature should be aimed at.

The ice-pail is almost as dangerous as the hot-water bath, "*surtout pas trop de zèle.*"

DECANTING

The transference of Claret or Burgundy to a decanter is by some regarded as a monstrous heresy, and as the weight of authority seems pretty equally ranged on the pro as on the con side, we may please ourselves.

I like to see the original bottle, not necessarily for publication but as a guarantee of good faith. Many good Clarets and Burgundies throw no deposit and therefore need no decanting. An electric torch thrust in the base of the bottle will show you if it is clear or not. There is, however, I am convinced, a great deal to be said for drawing the cork an hour or so before using, thus allowing the wine to "breathe." Decanting is a precaution against careless pouring of wine which has a sediment, and as the host is allowed, by custom and precedent, to perform this domestic operation himself, it is more likely to be carefully done than by the domestic who does not have to drink the result. A clean dry decanter at room temperature, a careful pouring down the side against the light which shows at once when the sediment is advancing toward the neck of the bottle which gives the signal to stop.

Many there are, not all of Scottish descent, who hate to see that half-glass of wine left behind. To those I plead that it should be poured into a separate glass and not mingled with the bulk; it can be drunk, if it must be, at the end of the meal when taste is a little dulled, or given to the poor, but a teaspoonful of muddied wine will spoil a glassful, and it is better dead.

A very crusted wine must be filtered, preferably through cotton-wool laid in a wine filter; but such things are Desperation's last hope, not in the normal course of life.

THE ART OF DRINKING

To get the best out of most things requires the use of a modicum of intelligence, and wine not less than others. For this also we ourselves must be at our best, bodily and mentally. All Smokers know those days when tobacco tastes like nothing earthly and should know the reason why. To wine we must also bring a healthy body and an alert mind.

We must also remove from its vicinity those things which dull or confound our appreciation. The palate stung by spice or ginger, cloyed by chocolate and sugar, is not in its most perceptive mood, and it is man who has brought these vinous enemies into an unholy proximity. As at first disposed, spices and ginger were located in the East, far from the home of the vine; Chocolate too, tucked away in South America, seemed safe enough. But—man disposes, and 1492 came and all its tangled chain of circumstance.

As the nose plays so important a part in the enjoyment of wine, we also ask that the room should not be overcharged with fragrance, whether floral or feminine; neither may the tobacco of either sex be allowed until the wine is finished.

Thus prepared we lift our glass, an eye upon its colour and clearness. All wine should be transparent and limpid; any approach to the opaque justifies rejection. The colour in red wines must be free from purplish-blue, a tawny brown denotes a Claret of desirable age. Tip the glass sideways against a white surface and observe the marginal colour, where the tawny tone will be most visible.

The first sip often gives an undue impression of acidity. Roll the wine over the tongue and its other components will come in prominence, aroma, vinosity, and strength. Listen carefully to the various notes, and after the swallowing no sting or acrid feeling should be felt at the back of the mouth, and the aroma should linger in the mouth. Consider the balance of qualities, with a scholarly frown, but do not deliver judgement until several sips have been studied.

One often thinks the second glass better than the first, one's faculties are aroused and interest stimulated.

This may seem rather like making work out of pleasure, but is not this the way to true enjoyment? Golfer, Cricketer, ask yourself!

If wines are varied there comes the need between each to put the palate "back to zero," and this is accomplished by something alkaline—hence the Vichy on the Frenchman's table. A crust of bread, a nut, or best of all cheese, perform this necessary service.

The best way to learn to appreciate good wine is to start at the top of the scale. Take a famous Claret of a good year, its merits are so firmly sounded that they are obvious to all. The fragrance reaches you before you lift your glass, the colour is of glass of the Middle Ages, the vinosity boldly defined and the balance perfection. With this as a standard we learn our first lesson; what to look for, and so far from spoiling one for lesser wines I consider it enables us to find their merits.

A Claret of the lower grades has aroma, but it must be searched for more closely and so through all its various qualities. Nor can we omit the power of memory to add to our pleasure; each of the great wines we have tasted have left their mark on our recording brain-cells and a lighter stimulus will set them ringing again, just as a photograph of a forgotten scene will bring to life the faded memory.

CLARET

Claret is the Beethoven of wines and, like all classics, does not reveal itself fully at a first acquaintance. An intellectual wine also, with a touch of astringency, perhaps a necessary quality for the preservation of classics. Richardson is forgotten while Jane Austen is still with us, preserved by the light acid of her wit and her gay, astringent irony.

Lacking the facile appeal Claret has lost some admirers, but it has the supreme quality of a classic, one does not tire of it.

No other wine can show us so wide a range; like Beethoven again, there are the gay light vintages of his Mozartian beginnings and at the extreme the sonorous masterpieces of the *grands vins.* And in between, what a country to explore! No wine is to-day safer to buy than Claret, and also none gives better value.

The practice of château bottling, that is, bottling at the château where the wine is grown, ensures that all such wine is genuine, and when to this is added the fact that all the famous châteaux only sell their wine under their own name when it has been a good year, we can purchase Claret with perfect confidence. The same wines sent over here in bulk and bottled in England usually cost 1s. a bottle less; these are equally reliable when bought from a firm of standing.

The four great regions in which Claret is grown are Médoc, Graves, St.-Émilion, and Pomerol, the Médoc district providing most of the famous wines. The four districts of the Médoc best known are Pauillac, St.-Estèphe, St.-Julien, and Margaux. Wines with only these names upon the label merely suggest that they have come from these districts and convey no guarantee of quality. They may be the product of a good vineyard in a bad year, or the average *vin ordinaire* of commerce. Purchase after sampling, if at all.

The next district is Graves, one or two of whose red wines are supreme.

St.-Émilion being more inland and hilly gives a richer and fuller wine, a half-way house to Burgundy it has been called. Pomerol, now classed separately from St.-Émilion, has wine of similar character.

In all these the most important thing is the name of the château, of which there are thousands of varying merit.

An attempt was made in 1859 to group these châteaux in order of merit, and it is still the accepted standard for to-day. The first growth includes Château Latour, Lafite, and Margaux, 3 only; the second, 16; the third, 13; the fourth, 11; and the fifth and last, 17.

After these come the Crus Superior Bourgeois and Crus Bourgeois, whose names suggest their use as everyday middle-class wines. Nearly all the classed châteaux practise château bottling, notable exceptions being Léoville-Barton, Giscours, and Pontet-Canet. This grouping of the wines, though done so long ago, is a fair approximation of merit, but in certain years a fifth-class wine may be better than a first-class one. This is reflected in the price, and a consideration of this point will go far to correct any vinous snobbery.

For the average person who falls short, like myself, of expert rank it is difficult to say how much better a Margaux is than, say, a Rauzan-Ségla in its best form. One may prefer the orchestration of Berlioz to that of Wagner. Some are very fully scored, rich, full, and sonorous, such as Latour, Lafite, Mouton-Rothschild, Cos d'Estournel (sometimes), La Lagune, and Mouton-d'Armailhac.

Delicacy, balance, and refinement, less heavily scored in the brass and wood-wind, will be found in Léoville-Lascases, Lascombes, Brane-Cantenac, Malescot, Desmirail, Beychevelle, and Cantemerle.

Turning to a well-known Stores List I see Mouton-d'Armailhac (1928) is offered at 50s. a dozen, Desmirail (1928) at 57s., Malescot at 60s. This year is considered to be one of great promise.

There is no other wine which can offer its finest at such prices, a guaranteed wine of a definite year, such as the first-named, 4s. 2d. a bottle! Compare this with the vague "St.-Émilions" and dubious "St.-Estèphes" offered by many vendors at equal prices.

The same catalogue offers 23 other famous Clarets from 60s. to 80s. per dozen and seven over this price. To descend in order of price we find two pages of Clarets, many of famous châteaux, but not bottled there, but perfectly to be relied on if the firms are of standing and probity. The prices descend from 60s. a dozen to 24s. to the Vin Ordinaire. A Cos d'Estournel ('18) at 46s., a Château Caillou ('24), a great bargain this, at 34s.

The Vin Ordinaire has no year, but I have bought Claret at 2s. a bottle many times which has five or six years to its credit. Springing to 2s. 6d., we are offered a Lagrange of Bourg of '24, and Bourg, like Blaye, though outside the sacred Claret areas, often produces a very good everyday wine; a '20 Côte de Bourg at 30s. a dozen I remember with pleasure.

Château Laujac and Haut-Listrac-Reymond ('26) at 30s. are good sound bourgeois wines such as one would drink in France as an opening wine, and it is a pity that the custom of starting with a beverage wine is not followed in England. The opening bottle is for thirst, to freshen up the palate and to awaken it to a state of appreciation.

Let us imagine a small economical dinner for four; we dispense with white wine and concentrate on Claret. The beverage wine is, say, a Laujac—two tablespoonfuls of which have been abstracted to put in the soup. After the Laujac we follow with a Mouton-d'Armailhac of '28. This with the joint or game. Allowance, a half-bottle to each diner; cost of wine, 6s.

But all these qualities, delicate or loud-toned, will be lost if Claret is cold; no wine is more easily depressed and sulks in the chill.

As directed in the opening remarks, a warmth not chilling to the hand is needed to unlock its secrets.

I can find in no book an answer to the question "How much wine does the average man require?"—a question of great importance. A bottle of Claret among six people is merely tantalising, a bottle each is a little over-generous for a mixed party.

Perhaps as a rough guide the following will serve: a quarter of a bottle—reticence; a half—sufficience; three-quarters—eloquence; and a whole bottle—benevolence.

It will usually be found that "the sober half-pint men and serious sippers" are the best judges; for the "Hey Nonny No!" School who quaff bumpers, a good bourgeois wine will suffice.

Claret to-day offers us the purest and cheapest wine available, and having strength enough of itself it needs no fortifying with sugar or spirit.

It is not without significance that when Claret was the common drink of this country, England was "a nest of singing birds." Let Whisky range her poets against them!

THE WHITE WINES OF BORDEAUX

A bottle with the sole word Graves, or Graves Supérieur (usually the same thing), is an excellent one to avoid.

Few names have been more vainly abused than this. The three witches in *Macbeth* are not named, but numbered. I feel pretty sure that their names were Graves, Beaune, and St.-Émilion. I may be wrong, but many hellish brews have since masqueraded under these names.

Graves is a less sweet Sauterne, but not a naturally dry wine. To have it at its best try Château Carbonnieux, for which you will have to give 6s. or so. If you like Sauterne but find it a little sweet, you will appreciate this most excellent White Wine.

As for Graves in general, the unhappy discovery that sulphur will stop fermentation and so keep wine clear has led to its abuse, and all cheap wines from Bordeaux that I have tried are ruined by this practice. Even the famous Pavillon Blanc from Château Margaux, about which much mystery clung, was still sulphurous after eight years.

For a cheap White Wine try the Moselles, the wines of Alsace and Spain; go not to Bordeaux.

SAUTERNES

These rich sweet wines are dessert wines and should so be used. Unhappily a tradition exists that they are suitable to accompany

Fish. I am glad to have the support of so great an authority as Mr. André Simon, who, in his *Art of Living,* resolutely banishes Sauterne from his list of Fish Wines.

Sauterne is rich and sweet because the grapes are very fully ripened, almost to raisin stage, and they are saved from sickliness by the wonderful gun flint flavour and aroma. To taste their qualities they should follow a sweet, or a sweet fruit, which has the effect of softening the sugary note and thus letting the other elements stand out in all their glory. Château Yquem is the King (or Queen) and is usually too expensive for most of us. Happily there are many aristocrats below royal rank. I have a kindly feeling for Rayne Vigneau, born perhaps of some wonderful bottles which once existed at the Château Trompette Restaurant at Bordeaux. Château Filhot and Château Coutet are both excellent and not too sweet.

Mr. Simon blends his Cox's Orange with Sauterne, and I agree if it is the January Cox; before Christmas they are a little acid. Apricots and Gages happily blend, and after a sweet of not too saccharine a nature, say a Bavarois, not chocolate-flavoured, they reveal their rich Schubertian sweetness.

Sauternes and Pont l'Evêque cheese should be tried; it will not be the first time that the Church has given the gustronomes a friendly lead.

BURGUNDY

There is a Gothic splendour in Burgundy which no other wine can match. It calls to mind the sun streaming through old glass and distant organ-notes and its music is that of Caesar Franck, that marvellous Belgian who found new harmonic colour when it seemed that Brahms had said the last word.

Wagner caught the true Burgundy note once or twice—the overture to *Die Meistersinger,* for instance, those majestic common chords made so uncommon by a touch of genius!

Burgundy seems essentially a wine of the Middle Ages, as indeed it was, moving with the slow majesty of those unhurried days. Aristocratic too; so small are some of the vineyards that the chance of, say, Romanée Conti coming our way is indeed slight. How can 4½ acres supply the world's desire?

Madame de Pompadour once tried to purchase this hallowed territory and failed. How can we, dear readers, hope for success, who cannot offer what she could? You may find Romanée in your wine lists, but Romanée Conti? If so, here is the tide in the affairs of men.

The whole area of the Côte, or hillside, where the best Burgundy is grown is quite small, only about 500 acres, and Burgundy is therefore an expensive wine and will always be, and on this account it is more imitated than most other wines.

Any kind of red wine, fortified by Brandy, sweetened by sugar, and edulcified by glycerine, seems to have gained the right to call itself Burgundy, hence cheap Burgundy is usually nauseous, frequently poisonous, and always to be avoided.

There is, alas! some wine from Burgundy itself which is sweetened by sugar and strengthened with Brandy. It is difficult to describe their palatal effect. The spirit makes its presence known at once in the mouth, the natural alcohol of the wine uses a more delicate method of approach. As for the added sugar, it is cloying, clouded, and muddy of taste.

To have a Burgundy at its best we must be prepared to pay 7s. 6d. a bottle and over, and one may well go to 15s. for the finest.

To my taste a "light" Burgundy is as a Wagner played by a "light" orchestra. Burgundy, like him, is all or nothing.

Following the method advised for Claret it is well to taste once a bottle of the Supreme, let it be Chambertin, Romanée Conti, or Clos de Vougeot. Throw all caution to the breezes and get the best you can.

Where, you may ask, is the sting, where that black curranty taste which we have loved long since and lost awhile?

You may be surprised to meet a fragrance not unlike that of some Clarets, a combination of delicacy with strength which exceeds the credible! This then is Burgundy as it can be, Burgundy "in all its sunset glow." Such knowledge gained, we are fitted to explore the lower slopes.

Here is Volnay, lightest scored of all its race, scented with a hint of raspberry and admirable with the paler game and the all-pervading fowl. Bossuet called it "a good funeral wine," and the author of the *Oraisons Funèbres* spoke as an expert.

Of Beaunes you have been warned, but an Enfant Jésus of eight years of age, with its wonderful bouquet, does much to redeem this slandered district.

Monthélie or Musigny are robust and long-lived, good fellows if not great ones.

If chance should bring your way a Grand Eschezeaux, a Morey, or a Vaucrins, try them; Belgium is a hunting-ground for such things.

And after Burgundy, not Brandy, but Armagnac; why, I cannot say, but they have the propensity of dwelling together in amity.

If a sweet liqueur is fancied, what more apt than Bénédictine, *in piam memoriam* of that great School of Saints who did so much to make Burgundy the King of Wines?

THE WHITE WINES OF BURGUNDY

Those who explore these wines need first of all a long purse and, secondly, a trusty friend in the know who can procure the genuine article. Like the red Burgundies, the imitations and lesser folk without the Law are in my view best left alone.

Chablis is one of the driest and palest of white wines and is immemorially associated with Oysters, but the genuine supply is so scarce as to be unobtainable except at a very high price.

Montrachet, the peer of the best red Burgundies, is even scarcer; ten shillings or more must be paid for the finest *crus*. Meursault is equally a wine to ask for when dining with a wealthy uncle or your publisher.

If we can momentarily forget the sordid limitations of price, then the white Burgundies are undoubtedly the best white wines of France; only, in my opinion, a few of the best Graves can stand by them.

CHAMPAGNE

Champagne is Art's greatest triumph over Nature, a civilised wine that must be drunk in civilised conditions; the Chopin among wines. We do not expect of it the elemental surge of Burgundy, or the austerity of Claret. To drink it throughout a dinner suggests a menu designed for ladies, no red meats or advanced game blend with its rococo appeal.

It is a drawing-room wine as Chopin was the supreme composer for this setting—a room, we sometimes feel, a little overheated and scented, a room in which the decoration seems to exist for its own sake.

After this I may confess that Champagne does not agree very well with me as an adjunct to a meal. As a tonic it is, of course, the swiftest and most pleasant of medicines.

Fortunately it stands in no need of praise from me, nor any guide to its intricacies. The well-known makes are "enshrined in English history and engraved on British hearts."

The processes of manufacture enable a high standard to be maintained, and by keeping to the well-worn tracks no disappointments await the explorer.

Cheap Champagne is a deadly potion, one that the Borgias must regret was created too late for their use. Nearly all reliable wine merchants, however, supply a reasonable brand of their own "reserve" at 9s. or 10s. a bottle, and in such cases no damage need be feared. For the classic names and vintage years 12s. to 15s. must be paid.

ALSATION WINES

I first met the Wines of Alsace in the Restaurant Alice, Rue St.-Roch, Paris, where they come to you in cool thick jugs as you sit, rather crowded it must be admitted, in rustic bowers over which aniline roses wend their weary way.

Since then I have drunk them as they should be drunk, in open-air bowers far from St.-Roch in the charming country around Metz, and what better open-air wines could be found? Of the Hock and Moselle family, poor relations, perhaps, they are welcome country cousins. With them we can indulge our more vulgar tastes, charcuterie, soused herrings, and strong cheese, which do not shock these sturdy rustic wines. I am glad that they are now to be found in England and we may stock the lowest grades at 25s. a dozen, so up to 58s. should cash, or credit, permit.

Riquewihr is the centre of their cultivation, and the principal grapes used are the Sylvaner, Reisling, and Traminer, in order of excellence.

There are Red Wines also, but I have never found these in England and rarely in France.

HOCK

There can be no two opinions about Hock and its musical comparison, Mozart, of course. The airy freshness, the horns of elfland faintly blowing, the simplicity which conceals so much art, are all there.

Who does not remember a first glance at Mozart's piano sonatas?

This is easy, said we, as we sat down to play. Alas! for the courage of youth, the passing years have only shown us what great skill is required to draw these simple outlines, to ensure balance and contrast of tone throughout the whole work. No! decidedly not so easy as we thought.

And so it is that Hock, so fragrant and confiding, seeming to tell us all its secrets at a first meeting, is not so easily comprehended.

Hock is Mozartian in its scoring; we must not expect the heavy brass, the rich tones of the strings which we find in a Sauterne. It is wine in the eighteenth-century manner, and we must attune our minds to its peculiar appeal. Set your memory on the opening theme of the last movement of Mozart's G Minor Quintet!

Hock can never become cheap, those piled terraces of the Rheingau cannot be extended. It is a lasting puzzle to me why Germany ever exports it, so small is the amount produced.

For a supreme Hock we must pay as much and more than for Champagne; great caution is needed with anything below 5s. per bottle. Beware above all of Liebfraumilch to which the vendor or shipper have carelessly omitted to add their names.

Hock labels always run a little to verbosity, but a few words are worth memorising.

Firstly, the Hock district is divided into the Rheingau, Rheinessen, and Rheinpfalz, the first-named leading. So much for Geography. The prevailing grape is the Reisling. So much for Botany.

The human interest comes in with the grower's name, Wachstum, Cresenz, or Gewachs, and his morality guaranteed by the word *Naturwein*—this is an unblended or unadulterated wine. If the grapes are specially selected this is denoted by the word *Auslese* or *Spatlese.*

The Rheingau district is the most northerly of all European vineyards, and its famous names are Ebingen, Eltville, Geisenheim, Hochheim, Johannisberg, Rudesheim. These are Hocks of supreme excellence, and one may pay anything from 10s. to 30s. per bottle for the most famous, and the fabulous year of 1921 established prices to match.

These we may leave to the experts and fix upon 1929 as a good, and not too expensive, year. These wines are quite ready to drink now, and to my taste adolescent Hock is preferable to middle-aged. At 6s. a bottle we can explore some admirable wines.

The Rheinessen lies south of the Rheingau and the wines are sweeter and usually more alcoholic. From here comes the famous Niersteiner, a name as often abused as that of Beaune, but when authentic is a winning creature who would lead the veriest Scrooge to a minuet.

Oppenheim, Bodenheim, Laubenheim dance with equal grace alfresco; in a mead of flowers, if you please, for night clubs and such dreary haunts they are misplaced.

Still farther south lies the Rheinpfalz, often referred to as Pfalz Wines; and Deidesheim, Dürkheim, Wachenheim, and Rupprechtsberg may be taken as some of the outstanding pearls in this diadem.

Very pleasant Hocks can be purchased at 3s. and 4s. a bottle, and so long as we are not too particular as to whence and how it is made; but for Hock at its best we must go into the teens of shillings.

Gone, gone are the days when Sterne could describe Hock as "a good wine for Curates." Alas! poor Curates.

MOSELLES

The Wine of Moselle has solved the problem of yet being light but not thin, romantic and not sentimental, eternally desirable, in fact a miracle which we all would fain perform. Sister wine to the neighbouring Hock, it can only compare again with Mozart, who performed so easily the above scheduled miracles.

Flower-scented as they are, the primrose on the mossy bank has been suggested; they differ from Hock in general effect and must be drunk when young, say, four or five years old, a point which makes for cheapness.

No wine is more suited to become an old man's darling; digestible, not acid, non-sulphurous, and no to-morrows in a dozen bottles. The Moselle country starts half-way from Coblenz to Treves, and the names best known in England are from the northern region, Berncastel, Zeltingen, Piesport. Just above Treves, the river Ruwer branches off and this small valley has gems of its own rarely to be met with in this country but highly valued in their own. Cassel, Ertelsbach, and Waldrach may be named.

Farther south comes the Saar, too well known to us in these latter days, and of these Wiltingen is most likely to be found in England. As their more southerly home suggests, they are bigger than the Northern Moselles and should be enquired for by those who like a fuller orchestra.

For the middle-aged Claret is, of course, the thing, but I feel that when I have more fully explored that land of Cockaigne I shall pass on to Moselle, and gracefully slip into a silvery old age with this good companion.

SPARKLING MOSELLE

Everyone has met, once or twice in his life, a crisis which suddenly brings him face to face with his innermost nature, and the encounter is a critical one for his self-respect.

Many years ago I entertained a devoted nurse at a lunch which was to celebrate a tardy convalescence and express my gratitude for her devotion.

After the food had been chosen I said, "Now, as to drinks, what shall it be?" "Oh, Sparkling Moselle, I love it." The moment had arrived. Should I, with unflickering eye-lid, order a bottle or, coward-like, a half for her and something else for myself?

Let me say I was still slightly convalescent, and after all—but I have never quite been the same man since.

Sparkling Moselle, what can be said for it? All that can be said for a Mendelssohn Scherzo, and little else. But can I be fair to this Wine of Dames? Perhaps not; the past haunts me. Why did I not say "Waiter, a bottle of No. 218," and damn the consequences. However, if any wine other than Champagne must sparkle, then perhaps it had best be that from Moselle.

PORT

Port is divided into two classes, valid and invalid, the former coming only from Portugal. The valid is again divided into Vintage, Ruby, Crusted, and Tawny, all of which are the results of treatment alone.

Port and horses are to my mind necessary complements; to dote upon Port one must maintain its antidote, the horse, or suffer in silence. Like all fortified wines it is "livery," and the only remedy is exercise, and equine before all. Other desirable accompaniments are Georgian architecture, Chippendale chairs, a noble cellar, and a dislike of all other after-dinner diversions.

In visiting a strange house one can always tell by a glance at the Butler if "THE PORT" will be served. There is a stateliness of movement, a sauvity of manner rarely seen elsewhere, save in the higher orders of the Church. In such houses one does not confess that one drinks Tawny Port at home, still less that your Aunt Martha finds Invalid Port does her so much good, "So searching, my dear."

No, we are upon Olympus and must behave as the Gods.

But Tawny Port drinkers have been greatly cheered by the news lately released from Oporto that the English Club provides, and its Members daily drink, a Tawny wine of great distinction.

For the Vintage Ports at their right moment for drinking we

must pay 10s., but with a good cellar and a reasonable expectation of life we may buy wines at 5s. a bottle to "lay down"—and what better stake in the country could one have? How pleasant to cast one's thoughts before sleep comes, on a few bottles quietly waiting below for their day of judgement. Port must so rest for ten years at least, and my readers may be able to work out the compound interest and see which is more worth while.

Crusted Port is cheaper and is a blend of wines which have not quite reached the vintage mark, but not to be despised for that reason.

Tawny Ports are matured in the cask, not the bottle, and so, like Sherry, undergo a ripening process of a different character. 6s. and upwards will ensure a good bottle from a reputable house, but as an experience 10s. or so should be ventured once in a lifetime, if not more, to see this magisterial wine at its best; there is no better foundation for a cigar.

Port has been blamed for most of the gout in this country, but with little justice. Did not the eminent Dr. Richardson say, "If Port does not agree with you then there must be something wrong with the Port"?

One fatal error is to leave an unfinished bottle and offer it in all innocence to a friend a week after the opening; nothing is more poisonous to some digestions. Wine exposed to the air for four days is as long as I find my interior will endure; and the same with Sherry, despite all I am told of its long-keeping character.

When a full bottle is not required let half be poured into a half bottle and well corked, then it will keep as long as needed.

Port is woven into the texture of our English life, and so long as our undergraduates are confined to their Colleges at night so long will Port be drunk. How else could they provide the broken bottles with which every wall is surmounted?

May it be long before Wardens and Deans become "Enemies to a chearful glass."

SHERRY

Sherry is a temperamental wine; in its young stages no one can prophesy what it will grow to, it may be the pale dry Fino or the golden Raya. Nearly all the Sherry which reaches this country is a blend fortified by spirit, and in this blending there is perhaps more art and judgement needed than in any other wine.

We have, therefore, no château names for Sherry but names descriptive of the character of the Wine, or its uses. Vino di Pasto, a breakfast wine; Manzanilla, from the Camomile flavour, Manzanilla being Spanish for this flower; Amontillado, the flavour resembling the wines of Montilla; Oloroso and Amoroso (delightful name) are names of blends.

Solera is the name of the mother cask in which some old wine is always retained for flavouring purposes, in the same manner as the Whisky cask, with the tap half-way down. We see "Solera 30," which denotes a cask thus numbered which will always be in being to give its distinctive flavour to younger wines.

For prices we may begin with a light natural wine at 52s. per dozen and even go up to £12 per dozen for old and famous wines.

Sherry should only be bought from a reliable firm; a blended wine such as this offers too much temptation to the artificer of flavours.

Pessimists may well note the gradual replacement of Cocktails by Sherry. Europe is finding herself again, and the erstwhile admiration of the raucous and crude is on the wane. Let us return to this gracious fluid with apologies for past neglect. We may take it before dinner and with the soup (although I like wine myself better here) and after dinner; rejoice, O ye Smokers, it may accompany the cigar or cigarette.

And as an inter-meal refresher upon occasion what could be better? Was it not Jane Welsh Carlyle who said that a "glass of good Sherry makes all cosy inside"?

HIGHWAYS AND BYWAYS

Nothing gives greater pleasure to the Wayfarer in Wine Countries than the local wines which he encounters. One is usually told that they will not travel, a story I usually disbelieve; it is the rustic method of avoiding the mental adjustment necessary to create a new outlet. When I find Anjou Wine at Calais I refuse to think that, given a calm day, it could not support the journey to Dover.

Of all the little known French Wines those of Anjou and Vouvray and the Coteaux de Layon are to me most worthy of introduction to this country. Nearer in character to Moselles and Hocks than to the White Wines of Bordeaux, they are gay, cheerful creatures.

In Anjou the Muscadet is to be sought; of Vouvray the Champagnised to be avoided; in the Loire valley the cheapest at the hotels is usually the best. The Coteaux de Layons sometimes appear in English lists; they are more golden and richer than the Anjou or Vouvrays.

In Eastern France are the Jura Wines; Arbois, so difficult to find in London, but so very good at the top of its form, and Château Châlon, white, is magnificent, not a by-way wine, a classic.

Tavel of Provence is quite transportable, and though I have never found it really first-class in England it is often obtainable.

Jurançon from the Pyrenees is a rich wine, almost Tokay-like, but it must remain a dream for Englishmen; the vineyards there require much finding, and I doubt if much even leaves the district; each farm has a small vineyard, barely enough for home use. Nevertheless you can always get it in South-western France—on the label.

A German by-way now seldom visited is the Steinweins of Bavaria, rougher and richer Hocks, but still flowery and romantic. We could welcome these sturdy flagons again. The red Hocks of Assmanhausen, Walporzheimer are for lovers of the "dry" worthy of a critical glance.

FRUIT AND WINE

Having now introduced these two excellent creatures, Fruit and Wine, we may venture on a few experiments in match-making, an occupation so congenial to the aged.

Wine and Fruit have long been regarded as suitable companions; we have the best authority, that of the School of Salerno, for such marriages. Speaking of the Peach the erudite doctors say:

> *Car la chaleur du vin empesche*
> *La grand froideur de la pesche*
> *Et la pesche par sa froideur*
> *Du vin empesche la chaleur.*

What could be more encouraging?

For apples, therefore, we choose a dry port or sherry; a fruity port or a young one are apt to challenge the fruit flavour itself. Or-lean's Reinette, Blenheim Orange, and all of this masculine group cry out for Tawny Port, the more highly scented Cox and its daughters a dry Sherry. The apples of Summer need less support; a Montrachet, if you can find it, seems admirably to enhance their daintier virtues.

Apricots ask for a sweet wine, not too alcoholic. I have suggested some Sauternes, but Mr. André Simon, before whose opinion we all must bow, suggests Monbazillac, that excellent wine of Périgord, but is not easy to find in this country.

———

Cherries have so far defied any matrimonial efforts. I must leave them in unwedded bliss.

———

Figs should certainly have a stout Mediterranean Wine, Sherry or Marsala are advised, and a few drops of either inserted with an eyedropper into the fruit before serving will win much applause for the gardener.

———

Gooseberries have brought me more criticism than any other fruit I have recommended. I am reproached by some for including them at all, by others for a too generous use of adjectives. Shaken, but not defeated, I still claim this popular fruit for the civilised dessert and for its accompanying wine, a Moselle.

———

Melons are admirable vehicles for art; with the cruet's aid we decree them vegetables, with sugar and sherry and various liqueurs we bring them to the dessert. It would seem that an unsuitable wedding is hardly possible.

———

Nectarines and Peaches were in St. Hildegarde's eyes but medicaments, but they have improved no doubt since they arrived in Europe and we now rank them high in our desserts. Mr. Simon advises Champagne for their nuptials, an excellent suggestion for days ahead; for the present I think a sturdy red wine, a Burgundy, a Châteauneuf du Pape or some similar self-esteeming wine is indicated.

———

Strawberries I have already married with a Claret or Beaujolais. The Strawberry likes a little roughness in its wooing, so a young wine may be used; the delicate fruit is quite capable of holding its own.

———

As for Oranges and their family, there is no wine that they will not ruin; let them remain in the nursery with the viscid Banana and bestow upon England's future hopes their vitamin beneficences.

—

Of Nuts it is superfluous to propose any banns. Port, Sherry, and Madeira have long been united with these in the happiest of wedlocks.

—

After a Pear, Wine or the Priest, says an old French proverb. If, however, your Wine is good enough the Priest may be willing to be present in any case. Pears are "cold in the third degree," said the herbalists, and to correct this wine was always approved by the leaders of the faculty. The feminine Pear demands a masculine Wine. Sauternes and the like are too nearly related in character. A Pomerol or St.-Émilion of sturdy character, or a Burgundy if it is available, admirably enhance and set forth the fruit's lighter graces.

—

For Plums and Gages I have suggested Sauterne, but Mr. André Simon differs and proposes a Forst or Deidesheim, and I think I must accept the correction.

The rich sweetness of a ripe Gage will be enhanced by the contrast of the freshness of the Hock.

—

Raspberries have so much fragrance of their own that an unobtrusive wine must be chosen: a Saumur is advised, and any of the drier wines of Anjou will accord or a Chablis might be tried; its flinty taste and masculine character should make a good background for the much neglected Raspberry.

INDEX TO FRUITS

INDEX TO WINES

About the Author

EDWARD A. BUNYARD (1878–1939) was born in Kent, England, where he worked as a nurseryman and pomologist. He is the author of several books including *A Handbook of Hardy Fruits,* and *Old Garden Roses.*

About the Editors

RUTH REICHL is the editor in chief of *Gourmet* and the author of *Tender at the Bone, Comfort Me with Apples,* and *Garlic and Sapphires.* She has been the restaurant critic at *The New York Times* and the food editor and restaurant critic at the *Los Angeles Times.* Reichl lives in New York City with her husband and son.

MICHAEL POLLAN is a contributing writer for *The New York Times Magazine* as well as a contributing editor at *Harper's* magazine. He is the author of *The Botany of Desire, Second Nature: A Gardener's Education,* and *A Place of My Own: The Education of an Amateur Builder.* Pollan lives in Connecticut with his wife and son.

DAVID KARP, "fruit detective," is a freelance writer and photographer specializing in fruit whose articles have appeared in *The New York Times, Gourmet,* and *Smithsonian.* He is working on a book of fruit connoisseurship based on the principles elucidated by Edward A. Bunyard, to be published by W. W. Norton. He splits his time between Los Angeles and New York City.

A Note on the Type

The principal text of this Modern Library edition
was set in a digitized version of Janson, a typeface that
dates from about 1690 and was cut by Nicholas Kis,
a Hungarian working in Amsterdam. The original matrices have
survived and are held by the Stempel foundry in Germany.
Hermann Zapf redesigned some of the weights and sizes for
Stempel, basing his revisions on the original design.

Printed in the United States
by Baker & Taylor Publisher Services